AIR WAR
PACIFIC

AIR WAR
PACIFIC

Christy Campbell

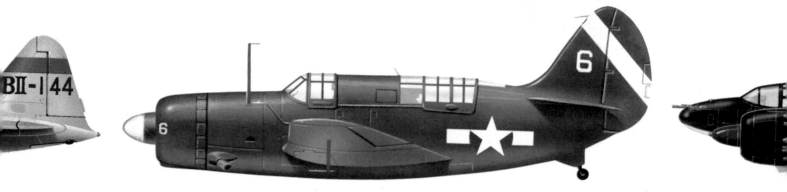

HAMLYN

Title spread (*Pages 2 and 3*)
Above left **Douglas Dauntlesses**
Left to right **North American P-51A Mustang, Mitsubishi A6M2,**
Curtiss SB2C-3 Helldiver, Mitsubishi Ki-46-III
Below **USS** *Saratoga*

Contents page
Grumman Hellcat

First published 1991 by
The Hamlyn Publishing Group Limited
part of Reed International Books
Michelin House, 81 Fulham Road
London SW3 6RB

ISBN 0 600 57070 2

Produced by Mandarin Offset
Printed and bound in Hong Kong

CONTENTS

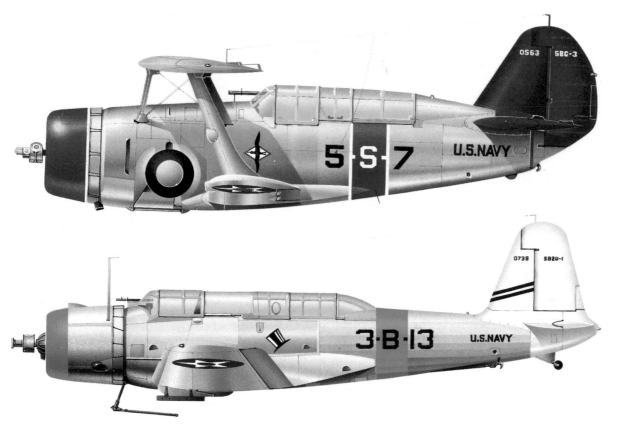

Top. The big, two-seat Curtiss SBC Helldiver, the US Navy's last biplane dive-bomber. It carried a single 1300-lb bomb and had a top speed of 240mph. Some were supplied to the RAF as Clevelands.
Left. Vought SB2U-1 Vindicators of VB-3, the 'High Hats' operating from the USS *Saratoga*, circa 1938. The Vindicator was the US Navy's first monoplane dive-bomber.

carriers. Both the Japanese and the US navies considered the carrier to be a very potent weapon and yet itself extremely vulnerable to air attack.

The US Navy, like the Japanese, emphasized attack. There were two principal ways of carrying the offensive to an enemy warship – by bomb or by torpedo. The Navy was also responsible for the aircraft of the US Marine Corps whose business was sea-to-land warfare and therefore air-to-ground attack. Marine Corps pioneers meanwhile introduced the dive bombing concept with the first of the classic US dive-bombers, the F8C-2 Helldiver. Dive-bombing was primarily a ground-attack technique but its adaptation to anti-ship warfare seemed an obvious next step, a well-aimed bomb from a plunging dive-bomber being able to hit even a fast-manoeuvring warship.

It was thought at the time that dive-bombers would not be able to pierce the deck armour and sink heavily protected battleships, but they could keep the defenders' heads down long enough to let the real ship-killers, the torpedo-bombers, come in from the flanks. The *Ranger* was completed as an all dive-bomber ship without torpedo stowage and, while the *Yorktown* was being designed, the Navy considered building her with an armoured flight deck as an anti-dive-bomber measure – an idea already adopted in the Royal Navy but which was ignored for another decade by the Americans.

Before the advent of effective radar, independent carrier task forces operating long-range aircraft needed effective eyes in the air – scout aircraft that would match the performance of the air groups, find targets and detect and give warning of incoming attackers. It was a natural progression to attempt to combine the functions of a two-seat scout and a two-seat dive bomber within a single airframe. In 1934 the US Navy's Bureau of Aeronautics held a competition for a new generation of scout bombers. The result was the

Douglas SBD Dauntless, the aircraft which justified the US Navy's prewar faith in the dive-bomber by despatching four Japanese carriers at the Battle of Midway in June 1942.

Torpedo bombing nearly fell completely out of favour. At one point in the mid–1930s there was only one torpedo squadron with the fleet, equipped with elderly Martin T4Ms, but the entry into service of the Douglas TBD Devastator in 1937 restored high performance to the torpedo-squadrons and revived interest in the technique. On the eve of the Pacific war the standard US carrier air group had evolved so as to consist of four squadrons of 18 aircraft each, one fighter, one dive-bomber, one scout (whose aircraft could double as dive-bombers) and one squadron of torpedo-bombers (which could also double as level bombers). Doctrine emphasized the offensive – which was to be made by simultaneous dive-bomber and torpedo strikes, the primary role of the dive-bombers being to suppress and confuse enemy anti-aircraft defences. Both the dive-bombers and the torpedo-bombers were equipped with forward- and rear-firing machine-guns, and the possibility that they would need to be escorted to the target area was minimized. The principal role of the US fleet fighter of 1940–41 was seen as the defence of the launch carrier itself.

The most modern US Navy fighter, the Grumman F4F Wildcat, had only just entered service after a prolonged development period (design had begun in June 1936): 18 had gone to sea with VF-41 in November 1940 aboard *Ranger*, and 31 had been assigned to VF-71 and VF-72 in December-January 1940-1 for service aboard *Wasp*. These three squadrons undertook a training cruise in March 1941 in the Caribbean, from where reports were drawn up about the new aircraft's virtues and shortcomings. It was fast and manoeuvrable but there were failings in detail – guns jammed and emergency flotation bags, for use in case of

Top. The first US Navy carrier was the USS *Langley*, converted from a collier in 1922. In 1936 she was converted again to a seaplane tender – and sunk off Java in February 1942. A second *Langley*, of the *Independence* class, was commissioned in August 1943.
Below right. The USS *Yorktown*, shown here shortly after her completion in 1937.

ditching, suddenly began to inflate in flight. Nor were these early aircraft yet fitted with self-sealing fuel tanks or protective armour. On the eve of war these deficiencies had been corrected and 230 F4F-3s (the aircraft was officially named 'Wildcat' in October 1941) were in service. Most were assigned to seven US Navy squadrons, VF-3, VF-5, VF-6, VF-8 and VF-42 (which were respectively housed aboard *Saratoga*, *Ranger*, *Enterprise*, *Hornet* and *Yorktown*), and VF-71 and VF-72 aboard *Wasp*. Two Marine Corps squadrons, VMF-111 and VMF-121, were based on the US east coast, VMF-211 was stationed with other aircraft at Ewa near the US Pacific Fleet base of Pearl Harbor on the Hawaiian island of Oahu, and a detachment was sent to Wake Island in the western Pacific.

Japanese Naval Air Power

The Imperial Japanese Navy had enjoyed immense prestige and political influence almost from the time the island nation began to emerge as an industrial power. Anxious to emulate the best from the western world and at the same time to adapt technology to new ends, the Navy ordered its first purpose-built carrier, the *Hosho*, in 1918. A British mission arrived in 1921

The Grumman F4F Wildcat, a shipboard fighter which served with VF-7 on board the USS *Wasp*.

carried reserve aircraft, not counted in their air groups.

The Navy also developed a series of light carriers, beginning with the *Soryu* and *Hiryu* of 1931–2 and continuing in wartime as the *Unryu* class. Typically, these light carriers would carry an air group of 18 dive-bombers, 18 torpedo-bombers and 9 fighters.

Impelled by the experience of war in China, and with more powerful aero-engines becoming available, in 1937 the Navy instigated development of a new-generation carrier fighter. The specification called for high speed, manoeuvrability, a heavy armament of twin cannon and machine-guns – and long range. The result was the outstanding, but very lightly built Zero, the standard Japanese navy fighter throughout the Pacific air war. Carrier requirements, such as the necessity for short take-off and compactness below decks, plus the need for great range determined the lightness of the construction of the Zero, which had nevertheless to meet and defeat land-based planes on comparable terms.

Inset. The *Kaga* was one of the largest and most powerful carriers afloat when she joined the Japanese Navy's Combined Fleet in 1935. She was sunk at Midway, 4 June 1942.

Above. **The Japanese Navy carrier *Ryujo*, pictured a year after her completion in 1933. She displaced only 10,000 tonnes.**

The first prototype was completed in March 1939 and on 1 April the aircraft made its maiden flight, with test pilot Katsuzo Shima at the controls. The A6M2 production model, with a more powerful Sakae 12 engine, began flight trials on 28 December of that year, demonstrating that the aircraft had far more potential than the Navy had dared imagine. The Zero's combat debut came more than a year before the storm broke at Pearl Harbor – in fact in the skies over China, where an intense air war had been in progress since 1937.

Top. The Mitsubishi A5M 'Claude' was one of the Japanese Navy's most important fighters during the Sino-Japanese War. *Below left.* The Mitsubishi G3M 'Nell' was used successfully in a long-range bombing raid against China from a base in Taipei, Formosa.

waters and extreme ranges of the open Pacific. However, in the opening operations in China it was the Navy which would lead offensive air operations, including strategic bombing, while the Army Air Force limited its activities to close support of ground operations along the Manchukuo border.

On 11 August 1937 the Japanese launched an amphibious attack on Shanghai, fiercely resisted by the Chinese defenders who pinned the invaders to their beachheads at the outskirts of the city for two months. Just 100 miles to the southwest was the city of Hangchow, the principal base of the Chinese government's small air force and the site of its training academy – a natural target for a Japanese air strike.

The sirens blew on the morning of 14 August, warning that an attacking force had crossed the Formosa Strait and was on its way. On the airfield were 18 Chinese Curtiss Hawk III biplane fighters which had just flown in from a dispersal base. With barely enough time to refuel, these aircraft, the 21st and 23rd Squadrons of the 4th Fighter Wing, commanded by Colonel Kao Chih-Hao, took off to meet the attackers. Kao's pilots were considered the elite of the Chinese Air Force. They excelled in aerobatics and in tight formation flying and had been intensively trained in air gunnery. The 4th Fighter Wing pilots had removed the standard telescopic gunsights from their Hawks, replacing them with crude but effective range markers painted on their open-cockpit windscreens and calibrated for a target at 300 and 800 yards.

The Mitsubishi G3M2 bombers of the Japanese Navy's Kanoya Air Division, flying from their base at

The Soviet-built Polikarpov I-15 biplane fighter saw service with the Chinese air force in 1937-8.

The Polikarpov I-16, although faster than the I-15, proved no match for the Japanese fighters.

Taipei in Formosa, had been in the air for two and half hours as they approached Hangchow: 12 of them were flying in a loose group at an altitude of 14,000 feet as the Chinese Hawks rose to intercept them. The Japanese pilots were taken by surprise, their air gunners putting up a ragged defence as the Hawks attacked from the bombers' blind spot, below and astern. Several bombers broke off and changed course, only one succeeding in penetrating as far as the target. The G3M2 dived through cloud to attack Hangchow airfield but its bombs missed the target completely. It was then pounced upon and riddled with bullets by the Wing Commander, Colonel Kao, and his wingman, Tan Won, and promptly blew up. The final tally was six Japanese bombers for the loss of no Chinese aircraft.

Later the same day, over Shanghai itself, a large force of Chinese aircraft, including Northrop 2Es, Curtiss Hawk IIs and IIIs, Breda 27s and Fiat CR 32s, took the offensive, committing over 100 aircraft to attack the Japanese siege positions on the ground and warships off the coast.

But Chinese success was short-lived. After aircraft participating in a series of raids on Shanghai were badly mauled, the Japanese carriers providing escort missions from the sea were briefly recalled to be re-equipped with new A5M monoplane fighters. In a battle over Nanking on 2 December 1937 Japanese Navy A5Ms decimated a defending force of Gladiators, Hawks, Soviet-built Polikarpov I-15s and

I-16s, forcing the Chinese to pull back out of range of the carrier-based fighters. To take the war into their territory, Lt-Commander Genda, air staff officer of the 2nd Combined Air Flotilla, proposed the establishment of forward bases actually behind enemy lines, with fuel and ammunition being flown in by transport aircraft. These special operations were continued until the fall of Nanking on 13 December 1937.

During the following two years the air war over China went the invader's way as the battered Chinese forces retired, still defiant and resisting bravely on the ground. Fighter-to-fighter combat declined, the Japanese air effort consisting of largely unopposed bomber missions. However, in 1940 the Japanese began to meet renewed resistance in the air. The A5Ms were not able to escort bombers to Chungking and back, and the Navy bombers were roughly handled, suffering 10 per cent losses on some raids.

The answer was the Zero, which made its first flight over the war theatre on 19 August 1940, escorting 50 G3M bombers over Chungking. No defenders came to meet them, nor again on the next day when the Zeros again made a 1000-mile round trip from Formosa. On 13 September 13 Zeros once more escorted a force of G3M bombers against Chungking, and at last were met by Chinese fighters over the battered city. The Zeros pounced out of the sun and, within 30 minutes, 27 I-15 and I-16 fighters

Continued on page 20

The Polikarpov I-153, one of the last biplanes to be built, had a retractable undercarriage.

A detailed view of the
Mitsubishi A5M, the
Japanese Navy's first
monoplane fighter.

報國-307
(航空計器馬

had been shot down. In the remaining months of 1940 Chinese air strength was completely broken by the nimble, long-ranged Zeros.

Air War with the Soviet Union

The long air war over China was the proving ground for Japanese Navy pilots and their machines. Prior to the outbreak of the Pacific War, the Japanese Army, too, was engaged in a much shorter, but equally ferocious, conflict – with the Soviet Union. On 11 May 1939 a minor incident on the ill-defined border between Japanese-occupied Manchukuo and Outer Mongolia (allied to the Soviet Union) drew the two Asian powers towards war. Border clashes rapidly escalated into a full-scale conflict, bitterly fought for four months as infantry and armoured divisions clashed along the line of the Khalkin Gol river. This second Russo-Japanese war, taking place in a remote area and overshadowed by the simultaneous events in central Europe as Germany invaded Poland, went largely unobserved by the world at large. However, it involved intensive and large-scale fighting in which aircraft of the Japanese Army Air Force tenaciously fought the Soviet Air Force (*Voenno-vozdushniye Sily* or V-VS) for air superiority over the bleak Nomonhan Plateau.

In early fighter-to-fighter encounters the Soviet Air Force was roughly handled. The Japanese monoplane Nakajima Ki-27s, flown by veterans of the China campaigns, quickly proved superior to the Soviet Polikarpov I-15 fighter biplanes and able to hold their own against the faster 1-16 monoplanes. On the first day of wide-scale air fighting, 26 May, nine Ki-27s attacked a formation of 18 I-16s, claiming nine kills for no losses. Two days later 18 Ki-27s of the 11th *Sentai* (Group) again tangled with a large formation of Polikarpov I-152s and I-16s, flown by Soviet pilots, many of whom were veterans of the Spanish Civil War. But the Russians misjudged their opponents, getting drawn into individual dogfights with the faster-turning Ki-27s – and again the Japanese shot down at least ten aircraft for the loss of only one of their own. The commander-in-chief of the Soviet Air Force, General Smushkhevich, rushed from Moscow in order to impart some Stalinist resolve into the Soviet airmen supporting the efforts of General Georgi Zhukov's 1st Army Group on the ground and at the same time to arrange for the despatch of reinforcements.

Above. Japanese Army Air Force Mitsubishi Ki 21 'Sally' medium bombers were first committed to action over China in the autumn of 1938.

Left. The Nakajima Ki-27 came into service in China in 1938.

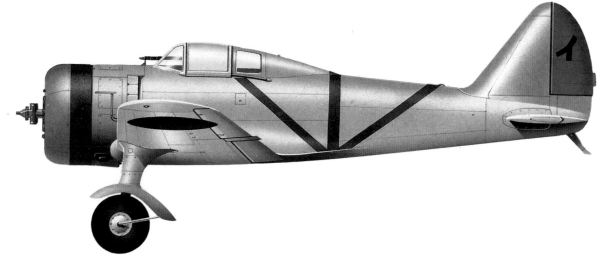

A later version of the
Nakajima Ki-27,
which saw action
against the Soviet Air
Force in 1939.

There was now a brief lull in the air fighting as the Soviets brought up new squadrons. On 22 June large-scale air combat resumed, when the Soviet Air Force sent nearly 100 fighters over the Khalkin Gol, catching the Japanese with only 18 fighters on forward bases. Large, violent dogfights raged for several days as the Japanese flew in desperately needed reinforcements. During such a fight, on 26 June, Major Zabulev, commander of the Soviet 70th Fighter Squadron, was forced to bale out of his stricken I-16 while over Japanese-held territory. His deputy, Major Gritsevets, landed his diminutive, open-cockpit I-16, taking his commander out on his lap while under fire from Japanese ground troops.

Control of the Japanese air war over the Khalkin Gol was exercised by a semi-independent Army command in Manchukuo – the *Kantoh-gun*. So far this had obeyed directives from Supreme Headquarters to fight only defensively, but on 27 June a strike force of 104 aircraft, including Mitsubishi Ki-30s, Mitsubishi Type Ki-21s and Fiat BR 20 bombers, escorted by 74 Ki-27 fighters, took off to attack Soviet airfields in the Tamtsak-Bulak area at dawn in a classic counter-air strike, aiming to catch the enemy on the ground. But the Russians scrambled quickly, the little Polikarpovs getting off the ground to tackle the Japanese army fighters and bombers. A huge dogfight began, with up to 150 fighter aircraft wheeling in the skies over the desolate plain below until, after 30 minutes, the Japanese broke off and turned eastwards for home. The strike force refuelled and rearmed, its target this time being an airfield in the desert 200 miles east of the Khalkin Gol. Only one Soviet fighter attempted an interception and it was promptly shot down.

Thus far the Japanese were in the ascendant. Despite its lack of pilot-protecting armour and self-sealing fuel tanks, and its mediocre armament of two 7.7-mm machine-guns, the Nakajima Ki-27 proved itself superior to the Polikarpov biplane and monoplane fighters of the Soviet Air Force. The Soviet air commanders drew on their Spanish Civil War experience, using large, fast-flying formations employing hit and run tactics, although the bulk of Russian pilots engaged were novices in air combat. The Japanese Army pilots, on the other hand, veterans of the China air war, were masters of the close-in, turning dogfight, using the snappy Ki-27 to best effect. The Japanese would try to break up the Soviet formations, tempting lone aircraft into high-g, manoeuvring combat. When a Ki-27 got on the tail of a Polikarpov, the outcome was a foregone conclusion.

However, on the ground, General Zhukov's well-handled Soviet tank and infantry divisions were pushing Japanese forces back across the Khalkin Gol, their actions backed by Tupolev SB-2 bomber strikes. On 21 July the Soviet Air Force launched a series of large-scale interdiction missions against Japanese supply lines, while more than a 100 fighters flew over the contested area. The next day Japanese fighters tried to intercept 23 SB-2s escorted by 120 I-16s. On 23 July a huge air battle took place when the Soviets attempted to swamp the Japanese with sheer weight of numbers – putting a total of 140 SB-2s and around 150 I-16s into the air. The Japanese met them with a force of over 80 Ki-27s and were to claim the destruction of 45 I-16s and eight SB-2s for the loss of only seven Ki-27s.

Fighting continued on this scale for two more days, the Soviets suffering heavy losses. On 25 July a new Soviet fighter type was committed to battle, the Polikarpov I-153, one of the last combat biplanes to be developed. Its retractable undercarriage gave it a good turn of speed and it was highly manoeuvrable and well-armed, with four 7.62-mm machine-guns. But the day of the biplane, however technically advanced, was over and the I-153 suffered rough handling in the air battles of the last week of July.

On 2 August the Soviet Air Force adopted new tactics, using its fighters to make mass strafing attacks on Japanese airfields. Japanese Army Air

A Polikarpov I-15 of the Soviet Air Force which fought over Manchuria in 1939.

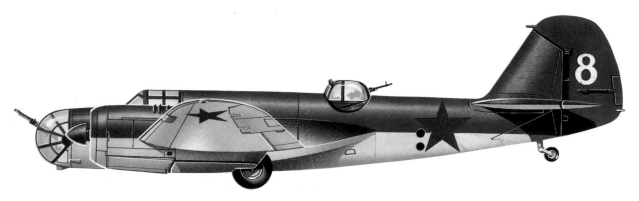

A Tupolev SB-2. The type was used by the Chinese Air Force against the Japanese during 1938-9.

Force losses on the ground and in the air began to mount and the ratio of kills to aircraft encountered began to fall rapidly. Sheer exhaustion was blunting the Japanese pilots' effectiveness as they operated against a numerically superior enemy, sometimes flying four or five missions a day. Some of the most experienced unit leaders had been killed or seriously wounded and the demands of the continuing air war in China meant that Japanese squadrons could not be rotated out of the line for rest periods.

Soviet tactics were tightening up. Big, stepped formations of I-16s would sweep in over the tundra, avoiding individual combat with the nimbler Ki-27s. If a dogfight was joined, the I-16 pilots knew how to use their greater level speed and dive characteristics in order to break off at will. The latest model Polikarpov fighters, the I-16 Type 17, also featured hard-hitting, twin 20-mm wing-mounted cannon, plus increased armour protection for the pilot and some form of protection for the fuel tanks, making the aircraft much harder to shoot down. The SB-2 bombers were now operating from high altitude – with less accuracy but virtually immune from interception.

After a lull in air activity caused by bad weather, on 20 August 1939 Zhukov launched a massive ground offensive spearheaded by no fewer than 800 tanks, which began to roll up the Japanese forces in a huge pincer movement. The Soviet effort in the air was similarly massive, with large formations of SB-2s, under heavy fighter escort, pounding the forward Japanese positions.

On this first day of the air offensive the Soviet Air Force brought a radically new air combat weapon into play, using five I-16s fitted with underwing launcher rails for the experimental RS-82 air-to-air unguided rocket. In an encounter over Buyr Lake, the Soviets claimed the destruction of two Ki-27s despatched with a salvo of rockets. On the following day they announced that they had brought down three fighters and two bombers. The Japanese now put everything they had into an aerial counter-offensive in attacks on Soviet airfields. The Soviet Air Force allegedly put up as many as 250 I-16s, I-152s and I-153s in their defence. During the first three days of Zhukov's offensive the Soviets claimed the destruction of 74 enemy aircraft in air-to-air combat. The Japanese admitted the loss of only ten.

With their front on the ground collapsing, the Japanese still fought tenaciously in the air, flying gruelling ground-attack missions, with crew fatigue adding to a rising casualty rate. The loss of experienced pilots was becoming critical. Their numbers included the outstanding fighter ace of the conflict, Sgt Hiromichi Shinohara of the 11th *Sentai*, credited with 58 victories. The situation became so bad that on 26 August the 33rd *Sentai*, still flying old Kawasaki Ki-10 fighter biplanes, was redeployed to the area from China.

In the first week of September much larger reinforcements arrived, bringing Japanese strength up to 295 aircraft, greater than at any time during the conflict. But by now the fighting was slowing down. Defeat on the ground (and the signing of the Nazi-Soviet Non-Aggression Pact on 23 August 1939) made the whole conflict look highly dangerous for the government in Tokyo, which was anxious for a rapid end to hostilities. On 14–15 September the last encounters took place, Japanese Ki-27 pilots again showing their mastery of air-to-air fighting in sporadic dogfights with Polikarpov fighters.

Who had won this undeclared air war fought out in one of the world's remotest regions? The Japanese had battled valiantly for four months with a numerically far superior force. Nevertheless, the three highest-ranking officers of the Japanese air combat group committed ritual harakiri, as did the few pilots who, after baling out over Soviet-controlled territory, had been taken prisoner and were now released with the cease-fire. Claims of kills made at the time by both sides were widely exaggerated. Modern research points to figures of around 160 Japanese aircraft destroyed in the air and on the ground and around 400 on the Soviet side. The Red Army learned much about the use of mass armoured formations and its pilots gained very valuable combat experience. The 'defeat' of the Japanese Army meanwhile was kept a secret – while the Army Air Force's 'success' in holding larger forces in check led to a certain complacency in planning new equipment and adopting new tactical doctrines.

Veteran fighter pilots of the Khalkin Gol conflict stressed the need for speed rather than manoeuvrability in new fighter designs with heavier armament, protection for fuel tanks (if not for the pilot) and the provision of airborne radio. In the fighting only one Japanese aircraft in each squadron had been equipped with a radio – a primitive and unreliable set. The Nakajima Ki-43, which was under development at the time of the Khalkin Gol air war and which would be the Japanese Army Air Force's most important fighter in the first years of the Pacific War, traded manoeuvrability for speed, but still remained undergunned and under-protected.

CHAPTER 3

THE JAPANESE OFFENSIVE IN THE PACIFIC 1941–42

The Approach to War

The temptation was overwhelming. In the autumn of 1941 the group of militarists who had seized the political initiative in Japan could look at the map of Southeast Asia and the Pacific and hardly believe the prize that was dangled in front of them. The German conquests in Europe had cut the French and Dutch colonial empires adrift and without any possibility of help from their homelands should they be attacked. Britain, with its Malayan empire, was fighting for its life and seemed powerless to intervene should Japan emulate its Axis partners in the Tripartite Pact and try to seize a new empire by military conquest.

However, Japan's long-running war on the mainland of China was stalemated. The effectiveness of Soviet ground and air forces, demonstrated in the fighting in Mongolia in 1939, had convinced the Japanese high command that the Soviet Union was too formidable and too big an opponent to take on.

Even as the Soviet armies fell back towards Moscow in the winter of 1941, there were softer targets to attack to the south and east. The campaign in China was the Japanese Army's war. If the high command should sanction the plan to break out over the vast distances of the western Pacific, this would be the Imperial Navy's finest hour – and its air power would be the crucial factor.

However, across the Pacific there was the still neutral United States, whose army was tiny, but whose navy was the largest in the world. And locked up in American industry was the power to equip the greatest armies in history and to build fleets of ships and aircraft that would make the Japanese fleet of 1941 look puny by comparison. For more than three decades the Imperial Navy had based its planning on

The magazine of a warship blows up during the attack on Pearl Harbor.

Above. **Southeast Asia showing the maximum extent of Japanese conquests in 1942.**

comparison with the United States. Throughout the 1920s and 1930s it had trained for a defensive war in the western Pacific against its rival.

Relations with the United States deteriorated rapidly during 1940. In July the US government announced an ambitious new naval construction programme. In September, as Japanese forces occupied the north of French Indochina, the United States imposed a trade embargo which included vital oil supplies.

It was, however, the simple calculation of future naval strength that indicated to the Japanese high command that the 'window of opportunity' in the Pacific would close. In 1941, as the Japanese Navy neared completion of its 1937 warship-building programme, there came the stark realization that by the end of the year it would stand at 7:10 relative to the US Navy. Furthermore, as future US programmes were completed the ratio would be 5:10 by 1943 and 3:10 by 1944.

Thus, if the Japanese were to move, they had to do so now. Simply seizing the largely defenceless European colonial possessions would not be enough. The Americans had to be knocked out by a stunning blow that would eliminate their capacity to intervene in the western Pacific.

The US Navy's power in the western Pacific hinged on Pearl Harbor, the great naval base on the Hawaiian Island of Oahu, first established as a fleet base in 1912. In May 1940 President Roosevelt had directed that the US Pacific fleet should be stationed permanently at Pearl rather than on the west coast of the United States.

Admiral Yamamoto, who had been appointed commander of the combined fleet in August 1939, described the presence of the US Pacific fleet in Hawaii as 'a dagger pointed at our throat'. However, the admiral added, the American naval threat to Japan from a base so far forward in the Pacific could be turned round – Pearl Harbor could become an ideal target for Japanese attack.

But how to effect it? Conventional naval thinking demanded a full-scale battle on the open ocean. Naval air power would be useful for scouting and harassing, but the final decision would be made by the battleships' guns. The US Navy would have to be lured under them.

An early plan envisaged long-range flying boats travelling the 5500 miles to Pearl Harbor from bases in the Marshall Islands, bombing Oahu and thus provoking the US fleet into a sortie.

But Yamamoto was not thinking of a Jutland-style battle refought in the Pacific. Fleet exercises in spring 1940 had demonstrated the effectiveness of attack by torpedo-carrying aircraft against battleships. Here was a means of not just provoking the Americans into war but of eliminating the Pacific fleet itself in one mighty blow delivered from the air.

In January 1941 Yamamoto drew a number of trusted colleagues into a secret planning group.

Admiral Onishi, an expert on naval aviation, began the task of planning an air attack on Oahu. He was assisted by Commander Minoru Genda, who as military attaché in London had reported the extraordinary success of the British Fleet Air Arm's attack in November 1940 on the Italian fleet caught lying at anchor at Taranto.

Genda's view was that a repeat performance against the US base was feasible but risky. It would need a force of at least 400 aircraft operating from all the Navy's available carriers. Highly trained pilots would be required to deliver pin-point, dive-bombing attacks using armour-piercing bombs against the decks of battleships – the primary targets. Equal skill would be required by the crews of torpedo-bombers coming in low and at slow speed to make horizontal attacks against the enemy warships' waterlines.

In April Yamamoto handed over the unofficial preliminary plans to the Combined Fleet Staff for further study. Four months later the Japanese Naval War College tested the plans in simulated attacks. In the first trial exercise the 'raid' proved a complete success, with four US battleships sunk, two carriers put out of action and one damaged. The second trial was less conclusive: this time the attacking force lost two carriers and 127 aircraft shot down.

The riskiness of the plan was already obvious to a group of senior naval officers – including Admiral Chuichi Nagumo, who would be designated as the task force commander. However, Yamamoto sold him the plan with his powers of persuasion, backed up by the threat of resignation. By early October the plan was approved and all the Navy's six fleet carriers were assigned to it. Nagumo now prepared his forces in detail for the epoch-making experiment.

Planning down to the last detail was all-important. Intelligence supplied information on the layout of

Oahu Island and its various air bases, including Pearl itself in the south, with its narrow inlet and sea lochs. In the centre of this broad natural harbour, five miles east of Honolulu, was Ford Island with its capacious Naval Air Station, used as a central maintenance facility for carrier air groups. There were dry docks, oil storage tanks and seven US Army Air Force bases – at Haleiwa in the north, Bellows to the east, Wheeler Field in the centre and Hickam Field flanking the base itself. Just west of the entrance to the harbour was Ewa Marine Air Station.

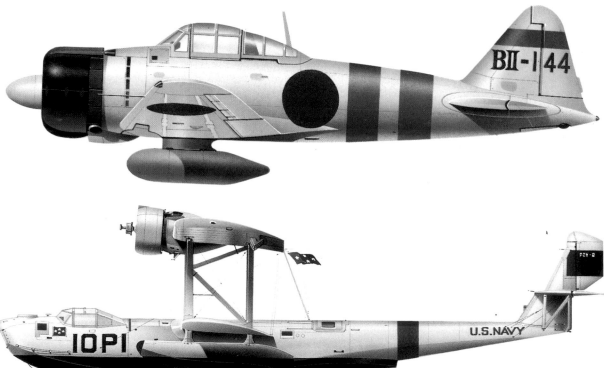

A Republic (Seversky) P-35A of the US Army Air Force based on Luzon, Philippines, in 1941.

On the east of the island was Kaneohe Naval Air Station, where PBY Catalina patrol flying boats were based. Extensive sand-table mock-ups of Oahu Island and of the naval base were created and flight crews were taken over them in conditions of great secrecy. The shallow waters of Kagoshima Bay were selected for live training because of the area's close resemblance to conditions at Pearl.

The big problem was the accuracy of torpedo bombing. Six months of training had been carried out by the Navy's best pilots but still the results were disappointing. Torpedoes were dropped too high or too low or failed to run true on impact with the water. It appeared to Genda that the low-level torpedo attacks would have to be abandoned – but Yamamoto insisted that the operation could not go ahead without the torpedo-bombing component.

The Attack on Pearl Harbor

The attack, codenamed Operation Z, was scheduled for 17 November. By the 11th of that month it seemed that the torpedo problem could be solved, but delivery of improved torpedoes fitted with wooden stabilizers for the short drop from the launch aircraft into the ocean was still delayed.

As negotiations with Washington continued the deadline passed, but Yamamoto issued a new operations order nominating 8 December (Japanese time) as the day of the attack. It would be Sunday 7 December on Oahu.

By 22 November the task force was gathering at the remote Hitokappu Bay on Etorofu, biggest of the mist-shrouded Kuriles, north of the Japanese home islands. On the 26th Nagumo's fleet of 31 ships slipped away from its mooring and began to nose eastwards. On 2 December Yamamoto's Combined Fleet Headquarters gave the orders 'Climb Mount Nikita', the signal to proceed with the attack on Pearl. The destination was revealed to the crews – the announcement being greeted with jubilation.

By 6 December (Hawaii time) the fleet was moving towards its objective at maximum speed, under cover of fog and radio silence. The last refuelling had taken place and the tankers turned for home. The main force was made up of six carriers – the Akagi and Kaga, the light carriers Soryu and Hiryu, and the brand-new Shokaku and Zuikaku which had just completed their sea trials. The battleships Hiei and Kirishima and the cruisers Tone, Chikuma and Abukama acted as a screening force. Already on their way ahead of the main body were 27 submarines.

Steaming on the 'great circle' route to bypass merchant shipping lanes and avoid enemy reconnaissance, by first light on the 7th the fleet was 230 miles north of its objective. The first Japanese aircraft in the air were reconnaissance seaplanes launched from the cruisers. The carriers shimmered with activity above and below the flight deck as engineering crews readied aircraft and armourers toiled to load bombs, torpedoes, cannon and machine-gun ammunition.

A Mitsubishi Ki-15-1 of the 1st Chutai, 15th Hikosentai. This reconnaissance aircraft was in service with both the Japanese Navy and Army.

Above. Mitsubishi A6M Zero fighters take off from the *Akagi* for the attack on Pearl Harbor. *Below.* Mitsubishi F1M2 Naval Type O observation floatplane, codenamed 'Pete' by the Allies. Its manoeuvrability led to its use as a fighter and dive-bomber.

There was light fog and a relatively calm sea — ideal conditions both for hiding the task force and for making the launch. Aboard his flagship, *Akagi*, Nagumo received in code the latest intelligence report on the target. Eight major warships lay in 'Battleship Row' but all the US aircraft carriers seemed to be missing. Where were the *Lexington*, the *Hornet*, the *Yorktown* and the *Saratoga*?

In fact the *Yorktown* was in the Atlantic, the *Saratoga* was undergoing repairs in San Diego, and the *Lexington* and *Enterprise* were ferrying aircraft to the marine garrisons on Midway and Wake islands.

At 0630 the first wave of aircraft began to take off from the Japanese carriers: 183 aircraft got off the flight decks in the space of 30 minutes. They consisted of 49 B5N Kates equipped as level bombers, each armed with an 1800-lb, armour-piercing bomb (converted from 16-inch shells which were fitted with fins). These were for attacking the battleships with their heavy deck armour. There were also 55 Aichi D3A1 Val dive-bombers armed with 250-kg blast bombs for use against airfields. In addition, 40 B5N Kates, armed with torpedoes, and 43 A6M Zero fighters, in three groups, would escort the bombers and make their own strafing attacks on ground targets. The reason for this large escorting force was experience in China, when Japanese bombers had proved very vulnerable to modern fighter defences.

The attack formations gathered over the carriers before heading southwards: approach altitude 6750 feet, above thin cloud cover; time to target 1 hour, 50 minutes.

The first wave formation leader, Commander Mitsui Fuchida, tuned his radio to receive station KGMB broadcasting its Sunday morning service of light music to Honolulu City. He was heartened to hear the local weather report proclaim 'visibility good'.

At Pearl the naval base was blinking into life in the Sunday morning mist. Crews were on Condition 3 alert. On warships one in four of the anti-aircraft machine-guns was supposed to be manned. On a hilltop above the harbour the US Army operators of a radar set detected the trace of approaching aircraft — a report which was interpreted as an expected incoming flight of B-17s from California. At 0755 the commander, Mine Force Pacific, on a minelayer at the entrance to the harbour saw an aircraft drop a bomb. He thought it was an accident until he saw the crimson *Hinomaru*, the Japanese national insignia, on its fuselage. Almost simultaneously with this, the fall of the first bomb, the signal tower rang through to

Inset. A Mitsubishi A6M2 belonging to the 12th Combined Kokutai, 1941-2. *Below.* The attack on Pearl Harbor was a devastating – but not a fatal – blow to US naval power.

Cincpac headquarters. Minutes later an astonished Admiral Husband E. Kimmel, commander-in-chief of the Pacific fleet, heard what was happening. On Ford Island his deputy, Rear Admiral Bellinger, broadcast 'Air raid, Pearl Harbor – this is no drill.'

Many of the crews were ashore on weekend liberty. One of the 94 vessels in the harbour, the USS *Nevada*, had raised steam in two boilers and a thin plume of smoke rose from her stacks. At 0755 parties formed for morning colours, the raising of the Stars and Stripes. As some sailors glanced upwards they saw fast-moving dots in the sky to the north – lots of them, ragged waves of aircraft coming in low over the canefield-covered slopes behind the harbour.

The first blows were aimed at Oahu's airfields. Bombs fell on Hickam and Wheeler Fields, demolishing rows of Army Air Corps aircraft parked close together as an 'anti-sabotage precaution.' Two minutes later, at 0757, the first wave of torpedo-bombers came skimming in above the wavetops to hit the warships in Battleship Row. Now the Zeros were pouncing on the ground, strafing targets at will, confident that no American fighter defence would come up to intercept the strike force. At 0805 the level bombers with the special armour-piercing bombs hit the battleships.

Some 60 minutes of mayhem followed as explosions tore through the naval base and great clouds of oily smoke billowed skywards. There was devastation in Battleship Row: the *Arizona* was wrecked and sinking, the *Tennessee* and *Maryland* were ablaze, the *Oklahoma* was struck by twelve bombs and crippled, the *Virginia* received nine, and the *California* three direct hits.

The only battleship to get under way, the *Nevada*, had been struck by a bomb and was beached. The old *Utah* had capsized. The cruiser *Helena* had taken five torpedo hits. Thousands of men were drowning or burning or entombed in capsized ships.

Then the second wave struck. At 0854 a formation of 167 aircraft, led by Commander Shimnazaki, arrived over Oahu. In the van were 35 Zeros protecting a force of 54 level bombers whose targets were the airfields, and 72 dive-bombers which would hit the warships once again.

American opposition in the air was negligible – the strike-force leader Fuchida did not encounter a single US aircraft in three hours. The destruction of defending air power on the ground was almost total. At the Marine Corps air base at Ewa 49 aircraft, F4F Wildcats and SBD Dauntlesses, were shot up on the ground by Zeros coming in over the mountains. Marines frantically shot back from the runway, dragging a Dauntless into position so that its rear machine-gun could fire. At the height of the attack a flight of SBD Dauntlesses arrived from the carrier *Enterprise* to find Ewa ringed by aircraft. Commander H.L. Young, leading the SBD flight, managed to evade pouncing Zeros and anti-aircraft fire to land at Ford Field. Ten minutes later 13 more aircraft from the *Enterprise* landed safely. At Haleiwa, the small and as yet unmolested army airfield in the north, two flights of four P-40s and one P-36 each, managed to get into the air between 0815 and 1000, claiming seven enemy aircraft shot down for one of their own. Bellows Field did not get an aircraft up until 0950,

Hickam not until 1127. Of the 231 Army aircraft on Oahu, 97 were destroyed and 88 severely damaged. The Navy lost 80. A few Wildcat carrier fighters flying in from the *Enterprise* later in the morning were shot down by ground defences as were four of the newly arrived SBDs, which tried to make an afternoon sortie in search of the ships from which the devastation had been unleashed.

The Japanese could exult in the scale of their victory and in the lightness of their losses. The accuracy of their attacks had matched that predicted in the many rehearsals. More than half the air-launched torpedoes had found their targets, as had nearly 50 per cent of the dive-bombing attacks and 25 per cent of the high-level bomb runs. The attacking force had lost nine fighters, fifteen dive bombers and five torpedo aircraft. Some 74 aircraft were damaged but managed to return to the carriers, now 40 miles nearer to Hawaii in rising seas. A total of 50 aircraft crashed on landing on the carriers, which were now rolling at 15 degrees; 55 pilots and aircrew of the Japanese Navy were killed in action.

The US Navy had lost four battleships. Three more were severely damaged and one slightly. Three light cruisers were damaged, three destroyers wrecked and three auxiliaries sunk or damaged. The Navy and Marine Corps lost 3077 men killed (including 960 missing, most of them trapped inside the capsized *Arizona*) and, in addition, 876 wounded. The Army and the Army Air Force lost 226 killed and 396 wounded.

With the first and second waves more or less safely retrieved, there was a period of uncertainty aboard the Japanese flagship about what to do next. On the *Hiryu*, the aggressive Admiral Yamaguchi was preparing to launch a third attack, but Nagumo and the 1st Air Fleet commander, Admiral Kusaka, had planned from the beginning to launch only two. Even though there were many vital targets on Oahu, such as repair shops and oil storage tanks, still intact, and even though the defences had been swept away, on the admiral's bridge of the *Akagi* the decision was taken to retire.

At Combined Fleet Headquarters in Japan, the news of the slaughter at Pear Harbor was received with jubilation. Everyone expected Yamamoto to

Above. Wrecked seaplanes and blazing oil tanks at Pearl Harbor's Naval Air Station caught by the camera shortly after the Japanese strike.
Below. US Army Air Force B-17C bombers caught and smashed on the ground at Hickam Field, Oahu, by the Japanese Pearl Harbor strike force.

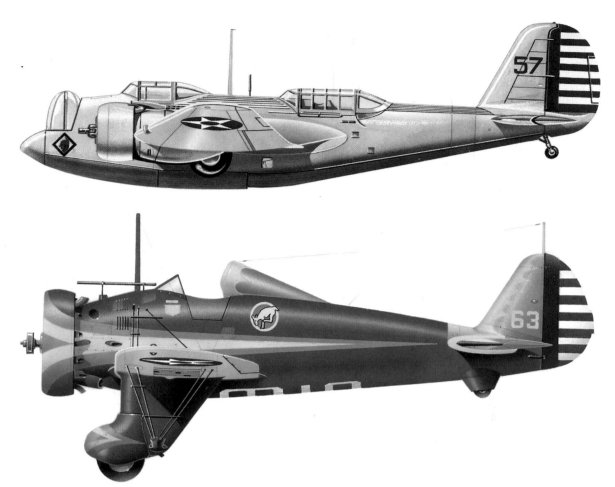

Top. A Martin B-10B of the US Army Air Corps based on Luzon in the Philippines during 1937-41.
Below right. The Boeing P-26 fighter was already out of front-line service in December 1941 but faced Japanese attacks at Pearl Harbor and in the Philippines.

order Nagumo to prepare a new strike that night or the next day in order to finish off the US Pacific fleet. Ever cautious, Yamamoto left the decision to Nagumo who, with equal caution, had decided, with perhaps as many as five enemy aircraft carriers on the loose (Japanese reconnaissance and intelligence efforts had failed to locate any of them), to call off the operation and turn for home. The signal to retire was hoisted from the *Akagi*'s mainmast at 1330, a mere seven hours after the first bomb-laden aircraft had taken off from her decks.

The attack on Pearl Harbor had lasted barely three hours. In air combat terms it was a masterpiece of air-to-ground warfare, at the very limits of what was then technically and operationally possible, using new weapons and skills to achieve an astonishing tactical victory. The defensive air forces were destroyed on the ground, just as they had been in Russia five months earlier by the Luftwaffe during the opening stages of Operation Barbarossa. The long-ranged and heavily armed Zero fighter seemed to be a wonder plane, sweeping all before it.

However, in strategic terms, although the attack was a stunning blow to US naval strength in the Pacific, it was a blunder. There was no warning, no declaration of war – a day of 'infamy' as President Roosevelt called it, that united isolationist America in a vengeful resolve. And the raid had only wounded US strength; it had not destroyed it. True, six battleships lay in the shallow roadstead with their superstructures shattered, but the carrier fleet, the real arbiter of naval strength in the much greater conflict to come, was still intact. As the Japanese

continued their drive to conquer the 'Southern Resources Area', to which Operation Z was only the preamble, American naval air power was still in being, able to intervene in the central and western Pacific, while the repair yards and oil supplies at Pearl Harbor itself were largely untouched, ready to nurture and sustain a reborn fleet.

Malaya and the Destruction of Force Z

The first shot in the Pacific air war was not fired at Pearl Harbor. A full 24 hours before, a British Catalina flying boat, operating out of Malaya and searching for any approach of enemy forces, was shot down by Japanese fighters. The RAF reconnaissance aircraft was shadowing a fleet of Japanese transports and warships sailing south through the Gulf of Siam, but their objective was unknown – was it Thailand or Malaya itself?

The British commander-in-chief, Air Marshal Sir Robert Brooke-Popham, dithered – he was under explicit orders from London to avoid any conflict with Japanese forces. But the Japanese were already on the move. What the Catalina had sighted was the so-called 'Southern Expeditionary Fleet', which had been despatched at the same time as Nagumo's Pearl Harbor task force. The objective of this armada, not a carrier strike force but an invasion fleet packed with the ground troops of the 25th Army, lay southwards – nothing less than the capture of Malaya. The Japanese had planned that the campaign would take 100 days, beginning with a landing in the Isthmus of Kra in southern Thailand, followed by an advance southwards through the Malayan jungle to capture,

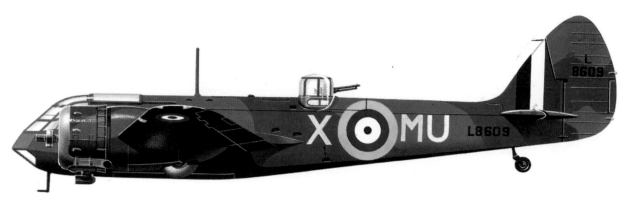

Bristol Blenheim Mk 1, the principal RAF light bomber, suffered severely at Japanese hands during the attack on Malaya.

from the landward side, the great British naval fortress of Singapore at the tip of the Malayan isthmus. In fact it took only 70 days and once again Japanese air power was to prove its devastating efficiency in this battle which effectively ended for ever the British empire in the east.

In the first week of December the Japanese Navy's 22nd Air Flotilla, commanded by Rear-Admiral Sadaichi Matsunaga, moved to new bases in French Indochina. The Genzan and Mihoro Air Corps, each equipped with 48 G3M2 bombers, took up residence at bases around Saigon screened by a force of 36 Zeros. Also within range was the 3rd Air Division of the Japanese Army Air Force which numbered 168 fighters, 81 light and 99 medium bombers, and 45 reconnaissance aircraft.

On the British side the RAF and its Commonwealth allies possessed 158 aircraft – a rag-bag collection of obsolescent types including Brewster Buffalo fighters, Hudson patrol aircraft, Blenheim light bombers and Vildebeest torpedo-bombers. Prewar planning had assumed that the defence of Malaya would require at least 500 aircraft.

Airfields were primitive and poorly defended. Seletar on Singapore island could count eight Bofors guns. The all-important airfields on the northern border had no anti-aircraft defences and were connected to headquarters by two telephone lines. On one occasion the air officer commanding was informed by the operator that his three minutes were up and was cut off. There were two radar sets in Malaya, but both were on the Johore coastline, screening the western approaches to Singapore. The whole air force was serviced by one maintenance facility on Singapore island. As the Buffalo, the primary defensive fighter, needed no fewer than 27 modifications to make it combat-worthy, this was not the most efficient of arrangements.

Following the pattern of the Pearl Harbor strike, the RAF airfields in northern Malaya were the first targets for Japanese air attack. Alor Star on the west coast, near the Thai border, was attacked on 8 December with fragmentation bombs, destroying all but two of No 62 Squadron's Blenheims. At Butterworth, on the mainland opposite Penang, an RAF counter-strike mission against Singora in Thailand

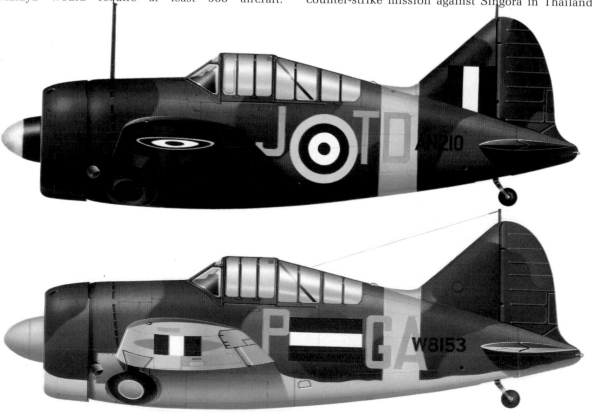

Above left. A Brewster Buffalo belonging to the Royal Australian Air Force based in Singapore in late 1941.
Left. A Brewster Buffalo with Dutch national markings, based in the Dutch East Indies in early 1942.

A Vickers Vincent of the Royal New Zealand Air Force in 1942.

Siam was caught, with disastrous results, as the bombers tried to leave the ground. Only one aircraft got up, a Blenheim flown by Flight Lieutenant A.S.K. Scarf. He hit the target but, in a running fight with Japanese fighters all the way back, was mortally wounded, crashing into a paddy field. His navigator survived but Scarf died that night, to be awarded a posthumous Victoria Cross. Five Hudsons and seven Vildebeests were hurriedly evacuated from the border airfield of Kota Bahru but not before they had tried to interfere with the Japanese landing there. One transport was sunk by bombs from a Hudson. Vildebeests of No 36 Squadron, flying in heavy rain from Gong Kedah, 30 miles to the south, unsuccessfully attacked a Japanese cruiser with torpedoes.

As the British position in the north of Malaya crumbled, the imperative to throw a powerful naval force against the incoming troop transports grew ever stronger. Force Z, made up of the old battle-cruiser *Repulse* and the brand-new battleship *Prince of Wales* had been sent eastwards in November to bolster the defence.

With the Royal Navy heavily engaged in the Atlantic, the transfer of any major resources eastwards was already hazardous, but a risk that Churchill insisted had to be taken. Force Z should have included the aircraft-carrier *Indomitable*, but she had run aground in the West Indies, leaving the force without fleet fighter protection.

Even so, the arrival of Force Z in Malayan waters on 3 December looked as if it might redress the naval balance. With the prospect of gaining fighter cover from RAF aircraft operating from shore bases, the commander of Force Z, Admiral Tom Phillips, decided to sail north in order to try to intercept the troop-packed transports reinforcing the Japanese

beachheads at Kota Bahru in northeast Malaya and at the Thai ports of Singora and Patani.

However, as the Japanese strengthened their grip on the north of the 400-mile-long Malayan peninsula, RAF airfields were being overrun by Japanese ground forces. Thus, as the big warships sailed north, observing strict radio silence, no protective screen of RAF aircraft rose to greet them.

But there were others in the area looking for them. Guided by reports from a Japanese submarine which had spotted the task force on the afternoon of 9 December, 53 aircraft of the 22nd Air Flotilla took off from airfields around Saigon to intercept them. Twin-engined G3M 'Nell' and G4M1 'Betty' bombers, mostly armed with torpedoes, climbed into a darkening, cloudy sky. For several hours they flew southwards through the darkness, sometimes dipping below the cloud, but without sighting the enemy warships. Suddenly one lead aircraft spotted two tracks of foam sparkling in the moonlight and the bombers gathered at the position of the sighting report, anxious to be in on the kill. At the last minute, it was realized that they had sighted the *Chokai*, the flagship of Vice-Admiral Ozawa's cruiser force screening the troop landings to the north.

Badly shaken by the near-disaster, the Japanese air commander ordered an end to the search operation, at least until first light. The weary bomber crews turned their aircraft round and flew back to the airfields in Indochina, having to make a hazardous night-landing burdened with live, unexpended torpedoes.

The two British warships, meanwhile, were indeed still heading north, through the soft, damp air of the tropical evening. Just as darkness was falling the *Prince of Wales*'s radar picked up three contacts

The Mitsubishi G3M2, one of the Japanese aircraft involved in the sinking of the *Prince of Wales* in December 1941.

– they were Japanese floatplane reconnaissance aircraft launched from Admiral Ozawa's cruisers just over the horizon. It was enough to prove to Admiral Phillips that all chance of catching the Japanese invasion force by surprise and undefended had gone. At 2015 he reluctantly swung the task force south – back to Singapore.

Just before midnight there came a signal from Phillip's chief-of-staff, Admiral Palliser, who was shore-based in Singapore. It read 'Enemy reported landing Kuantan'. This was a coastal town 200 miles to the north of the naval fortress. Admiral Phillips swung westwards to intercept, anxious to obtain some results from his sortie.

He did not signal his change of direction nor did he request air cover. Arriving off Kuantan in daylight, the warships saw no apparent Japanese activity. The report seemed like a false alarm – straying water buffaloes had detonated a minefield – but the ships steamed slowly down the coast for several hours to make sure.

However, they were being stalked again by a Japanese submarine which had spotted the change of course and had radioed air fleet headquarters. At first light Japanese reconnaissance aircraft had been despatched to find them, while the bombers which had returned from their abortive mission the night before were refuelled for a second attempt.

Even though the exact position of the targets was still unknown, early on 10 December, 94 bombers rose from their bases. Visibility was good, with broken cloud cover, and the torpedo-armed G3Ms and G4Ms climbed to 10,000 feet where, in formations of nine, they settled on a southerly course, eagerly awaiting a target sighting from the reconnaissance aircraft ahead of them.

The Japanese formation skirted the Malayan coast widely, wary of fighter interception which never in fact happened. They flew southwards almost as far as Singapore itself, but sighted nothing. Fuel was running low and the lead aircraft were already turning round back to Saigon.

Suddenly there came a sighting report: 'two enemy battleships, 70 nautical miles southeast of Kuantan'. As cloud cover broke beneath the formation, there, below them in the blue waters of the South China Sea were two capital ships. No mistake this time – it was the enemy.

Eight G3M Nells went in first, sweeping low over the *Repulse* and straddling her with bombs, one of which struck her starboard side but did little damage. The torpedo aircraft concentrated first on the bigger *Prince of Wales*, coming in very fast and low, apparently immune to the battleship's own anti-aircraft fire. Nine torpedoes were launched, two of which struck home, critically damaging the ship's steering gear and snapping one propeller shaft. With electrical power now lacking, the crew of the mortally wounded ship fought valiantly to keep her guns in action against their tormentors.

Two waves of torpedo aircraft now attacked the *Repulse*. The battlecruiser twisted and turned and, miraculously, managed to dodge every one of the torpedoes. The ship's commander, Captain Tennant, broke radio silence, telling Singapore of Force Z's plight and requesting immediate fighter assistance.

The *Prince of Wales* leaves Singapore on 8 December 1941 on its last journey.

The battlecruiser *Repulse*, which was sunk together with the *Prince of Wales*.

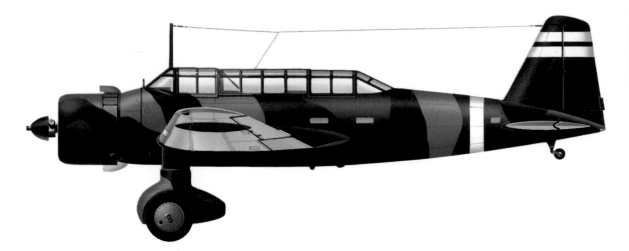

The Mitsubishi Ki-30 first saw service in China in 1938 but proved vulnerable in the Pacific war without fighter escort.

At Semwabang airfield, 11 RAF Brewster Buffaloes of 453 Squadron took off, led by Flight Lieutenant T.A. Vigors, but they were at least an hour's flying time away from the life-or-death struggle between warships and aircraft which was about to reach its climax.

The *Prince of Wales* was losing the fight. Six G4M1 Bettys attacked the ship, now without steering and with her anti-aircraft guns having to be laid by hand and firing only fitfully. Four torpedoes struck the starboard, one of them going right through the bow and out the other side.

Four miles away the *Repulse's* luck was about to run out. Eight G4M1s attacked her from the starboard quarter, and again Tennant was able to avoid the torpedo tracks by his brilliant handling of the ship. But a single torpedo launched from the port side struck her amidships. Nine more torpedo-bombers now swarmed in from all directions, four torpedoes striking home. Just 11 minutes after the first torpedo struck her, at 1233 the *Repulse* rolled over and sank, 796 men including her commander being rescued by

destroyers.

The *Prince of Wales* was finished, her steering smashed, lying virtually dead in the water. The Japanese departed the scene, their deadly work done. At 1320 the battleship rolled over, with Admiral Phillips still on the bridge. For a few minutes she floated upside down, then her bow reared up and the great ship slid stern first to the bottom. Three minutes earlier the first RAF fighter had arrived, to find an empty sky and nothing to do except circle mournfully over the scene of desolation, as destroyers struggled to pick up survivors.

No Japanese surface warship had been involved in the annihilation of Force Z. The destruction of British naval power in the Far East by land-based aircraft, following so closely on the shattering of the US Pacific fleet by carrier-based aircraft, was a stunning blow for the new Allies. A surface fleet without air cover was seen to be a tragically vulnerable anachronism. The United States and Britain would have to learn hard and learn quickly.

A Nakajima B5N1, armed with an air-launched Long Lance torpedo, takes off from a Japanese Navy carrier.

A dawn attack by Douglas Dauntless bombers. Wake Island lies below.

Wake, the Philippines, the Java Sea and Darwin

Pearl Harbor was a set-piece massacre of a fleet in harbour, the result of months of planning. The destruction of Force Z was a brilliant piece of improvisation resulting in something quite unprecedented – the sinking of battleships on the open ocean by aircraft alone. Both actions had, in Winston Churchill's words, left 'no British or American capital ships in the Indian Ocean or the Pacific ... over this vast expanse of waters Japan was supreme, and we everywhere were weak and naked.'

The Japanese were moving fast to exploit this weakness, striking out over a vast area with naval air power spearheading each attack. Hong Kong was overrun from the Chinese mainland, falling on

Christmas Day. The US-garrisoned islands of Guam and Wake were attacked. On 10 December a handful of US marines and sailors were quickly overwhelmed on Guam, but Wake proved a tougher nut to crack.

The island had been developed in the 1930s as an aircraft staging post for Pan American Airways. Its defences were scant. The garrison of 500 marines had a few 5-inch coast-defence guns and some heavy machine-guns. There were, however, 12 Grumman F4F-3 Wildcats of Marine Fighting Squadron 21, commanded by Major Paul Putnam. They had been ferried in by the USS Enterprise (which had thus escaped the debacle at Pearl Harbor) on 4 December. But few of the Marine Corps pilots had flown the Wildcat before and only two of the aircraft had

Continued on page 42

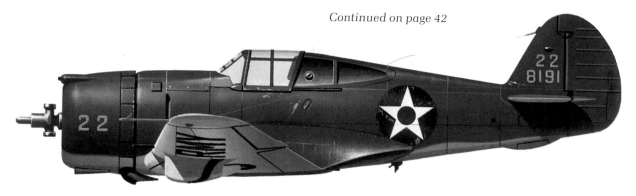

A Curtiss P-36C of the US Army Air Force in 1942.

The Nakajima Ki-43
was very effective in
the early stages of the
Pacific war, but could
not compete with
more advanced Allied
fighters.

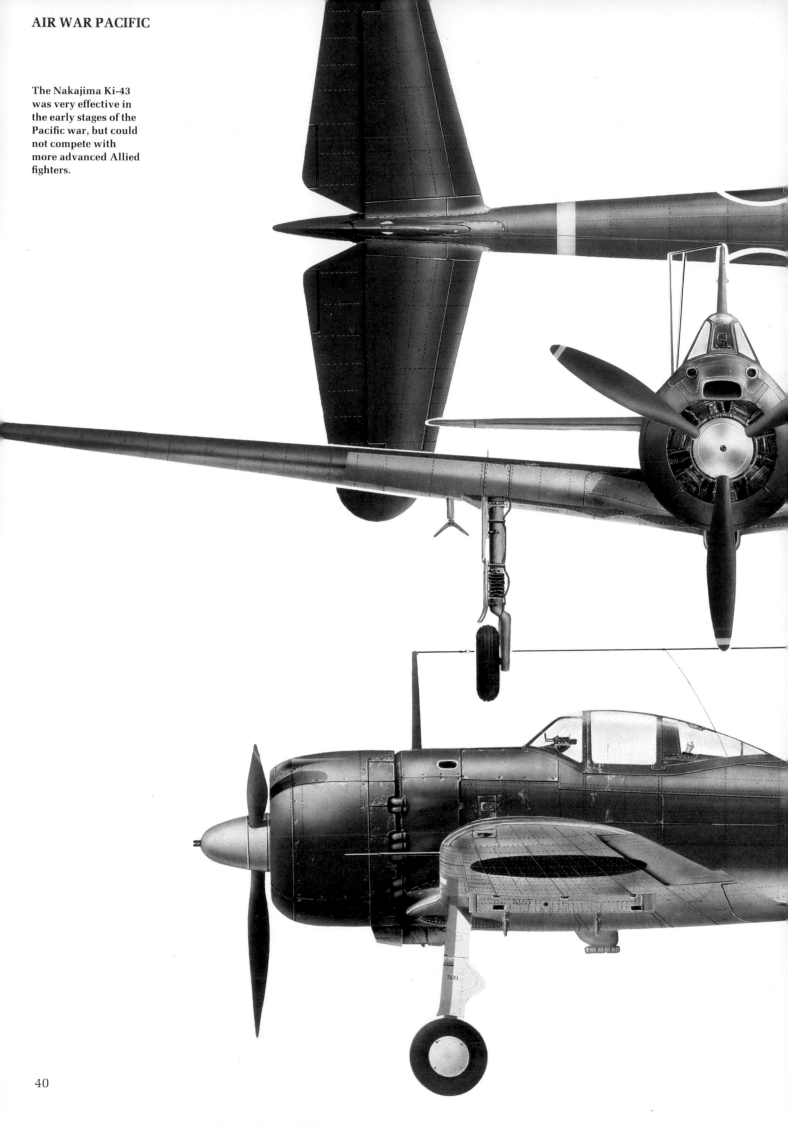

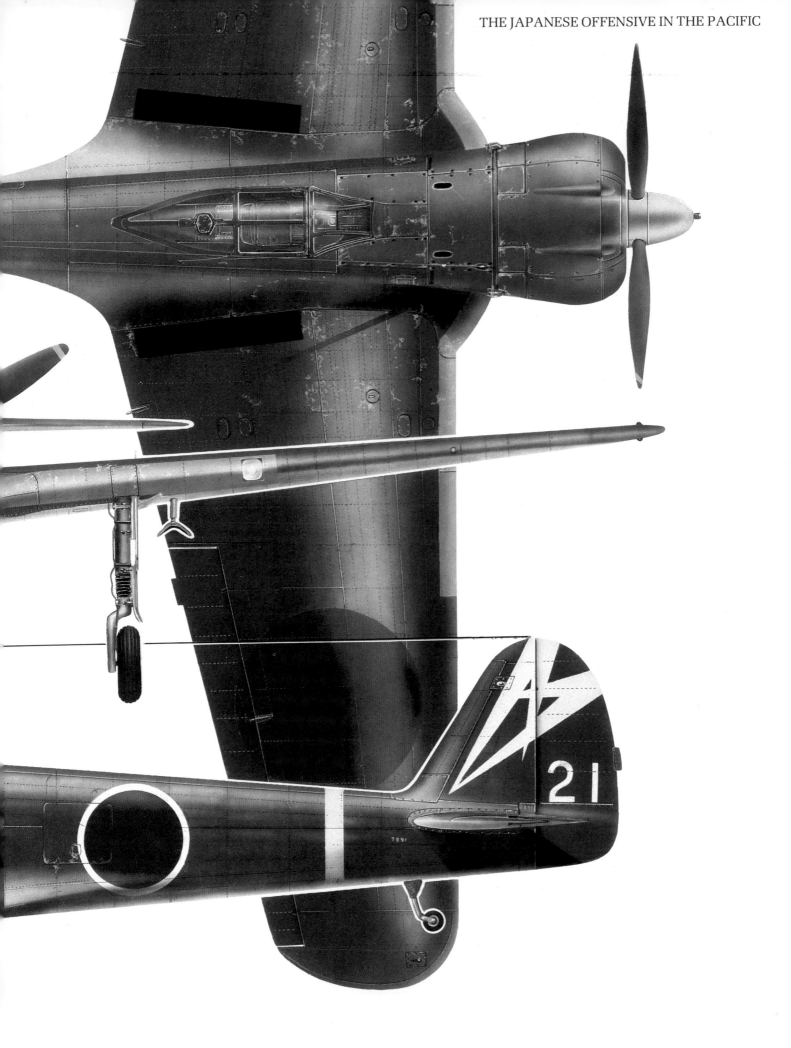

I. Hasegawa

From a wartime newsreel – a Japanese aircraft takes off from a carrier.

self-sealing fuel tanks (and thus were prone to blow up if hit). Moreover, the 100-lb bombs stockpiled on Wake did not fit the Wildcat's bomb rack. There were no revetments to shelter the aircraft from air attack, no ground equipment, no radar, fighter control centre or fire control equipment – just an observation post on top of a water tank.

On 8 December, under cover of rain squalls, 36 Japanese bombers swept in low over the island and destroyed seven F4Fs on the ground. After two more days of air attack an invasion force of warships and transports arrived to assault the island directly. This was beaten off by accurate fire from the shore batteries and by four of the five surviving Wildcats. The tubby little F4Fs hurled themselves at the invaders, dropping light 100-lb bombs and making strafing attacks. Amazingly, they inflicted damage on two light cruisers and sank the destroyer *Kisavagi*. Two Wildcats were lost in this action and all had been shot down by 22 December, having bravely resisted air assaults by land-based bombers and carrier aircraft.

With no fighter protection the garrison was wide open to a ruthless air and naval gun bombardment. At 0730 on the 23rd, with his forces heavily outnumbered, Wake's commander, Major James Devereux of the US Marine Corps, surrendered.

The Philippines

Operations against the US-garrisoned Philippines began as the battleships in Pearl Harbor were still blazing. Again, the primary target of Japanese air power was the airfields. Much of the American

planning for the defence of the sprawling mass of islands against naval attack hinged on the use of land-based bombers. Major-General Lewis H. Brereton, commanding the US Far East Air Force, could count 35 brand-new B-17s in his order of battle. Their mission would be to attack warships far out to sea. But to effect this or even to make counter-strikes against the Japanese 11th Air Fleet's bases on Formosa, his strategic air reserve needed accurate intelligence and a fast-footed response. This, however, was as lacking in the Philippines as it had been in Hawaii.

The first indication of what was happening at Pearl Harbor reached the Philippine capital, Manila, at 0230 local time (0800 Hawaiian time) on 7 December. Even though Brereton had been warned by Washington that an attack was imminent, the first Japanese blows, aimed at satellite airfields in northern Luzon, were unopposed. Three hours later, at 1235, 8 December, the main attack force materialized, catching US Army Air Force aircraft on the ground, their crews at lunch or servicing their aircraft. Flying from Formosa, 14 Japanese Army Air Force heavy bombers struck airfields in northern Luzon, while 18 twin-engined light bombers hit Tuguaroa airfield in the centre of the island. Some 192 Japanese naval aircraft of the 11th Air Fleet, also flying from Formosa, hit Clark and Nichols Fields. The US 3rd Pursuit Squadron managed to get airborne. However, all but two of its planes were shot out of the air by Zeros. On 10 December the naval base at Cavite near Manila was attacked by bombers operating at high altitude, well clear of its

A Curtiss P-40 Warhawk of 36th Squadron, US Army Air Force, 1941.

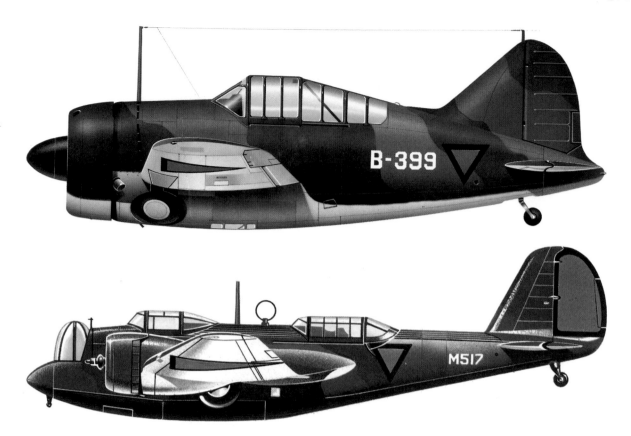

Top right. **A Brewster B-399D of the Netherlands East Indies Army Air Corps, based in the Dutch East Indies in 1941.**
Below right. **A Martin 139WH2 of the Royal Netherlands Indies Army Air Corps in 1941.**

outmoded anti-aircraft defences.

It was not just the fighter defences which were hit. For a week before the attack the PBY Catalinas of Patrol Wing 10, commanded by Captain Wagner, had been patrolling ceaselessly, following up every rumour of a Japanese ship sighting. Ordered to avoid detection where possible, the PBY crews had nevertheless encountered Japanese search aircraft which occasionally made dummy attack runs. Now the war was on in earnest and the PBYs were dispersed to remote lakes and mangrove swamps while the seaplane tender, the USS *Childs*, remained in Manila Bay.

As the onslaught fell on the Philippines, the patrol squadrons made what contribution they could. On 9 December two cargo ships were attacked – a Japanese freighter and a Norwegian steamer which failed to respond to a challenge. One PBY disappeared on patrol and two more were damaged – one by enemy fighters and the other by 'friendly' anti-aircraft fire.

Five PBYs from Manila attacked a force of Japanese warships on the following day. A strike with torpedoes planned for later that day was abandoned when Zeros swept in low over the base at Olongapo just as the US naval aircraft were about to take off, and Patrol Wing 10 lost another two planes. Commander Gray of the Olongapo squadron sent out all seven surviving PBYs on the morning of 12 December, having received (baseless) reports that a Japanese carrier force was steaming down the coast of Luzon. After a fruitless search, low on fuel and with exhausted crews, the PBYs were being shadowed by Zeros. As they returned to their base and were moored, the Zeros pounced, shooting them all up. Mercifully their crews had just got ashore in time.

By now General Brereton had only 33 Army Air Force fighters left. The fate of the PBYs at Olongapo showed that unescorted patrols were tempting fate. By now, reduced to barely squadron strength, while a few slightly damaged aircraft remained at Mariveles, the rest of Patrol Wing 10 headed south, refuelling at Lake Lano on Mindanao. On 18 December they departed for Menado in the north of the Celebes to join the tender, the USS *Childs*.

On the 14th the US Army Air Force managed to scrape together five B-17s to attack enemy ships at

Continued on page 48

A Curtiss Hawk 75A-7 of the Royal Netherlands Indies Air Force based at Madioen, Dutch East Indies, in December 1941.

The Grumman F6F
Hellcat was the US
Navy's most
outstanding fighter
during the Pacific war.

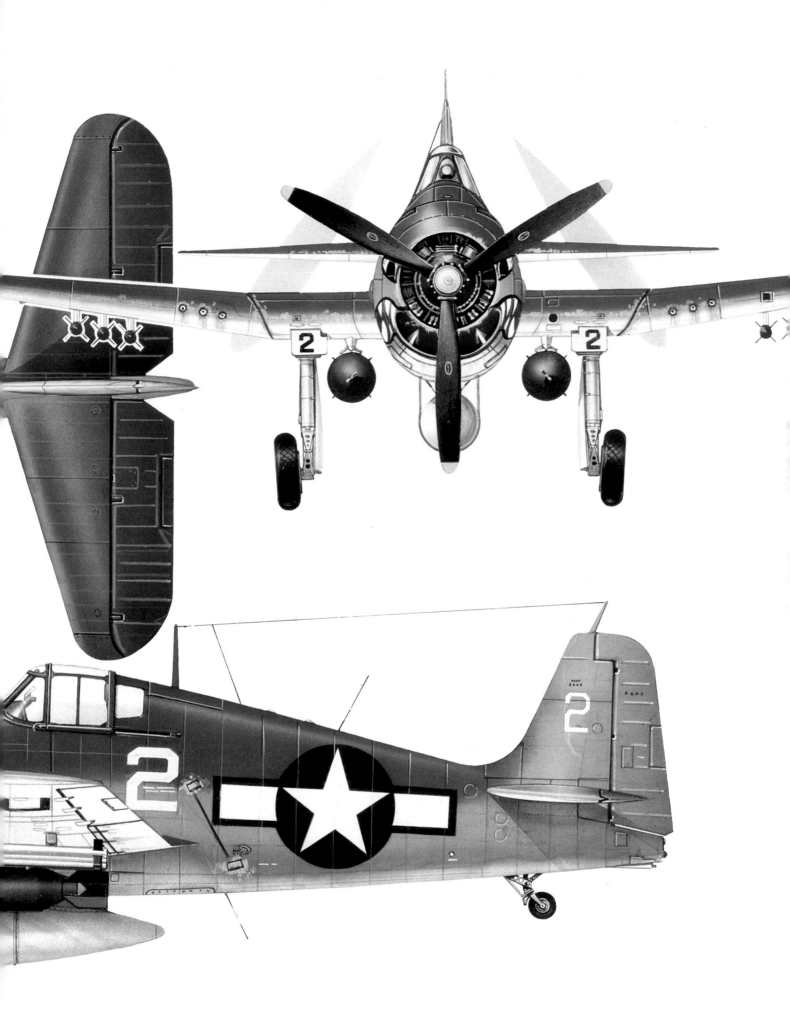

Douglas SBD Dauntless dive-bombers of Bomber-Scout squadron VS-6 over the USS *Enterprise*, shortly before the outbreak of the Pacific war.

Above. An American Volunteer Group armourer works on a Curtiss P-40 of the Flying Tigers.

Legaspi harbour in southern Luzon. Three got through and one of them managed to straddle a minesweeper with bombs, but the aircraft, piloted by Captain H.T. Wheels, was shot up by Zeros on the return flight in a running fight lasting an hour which killed the radio operator, wounded two gunners and knocked out two engines. Three days later there were only 14 B-17s left in the entire Philippines. They were subsequently flown out to the comparative safety of Bachelor Field, near Darwin, Australia, as US ground forces retreated into the Bataan peninsula to make a last stand.

The Java Sea

Bypassing the besieged defenders of Singapore and Bataan, Japanese air, sea and land forces continued to fan out southwards into the Dutch East Indies, brushing aside a defence thrown together by the newly constituted ABDA (American-British-Dutch-Australian) Allied Command. In the Java Sea an attempt by the Allies to dispute the Japanese landing resulted in the loss of two cruisers and three destroyers. Surviving Allied warships to the north were hunted down and quickly despatched, while to the south Japanese carrier aircraft sank 175,000 tons of Allied shipping and various warships trying to escape from Java. Among the casualties was the old seaplane tender, the USS *Langley*, which had been the US Navy's first aircraft carrier, caught at sea while attempting to ferry a load of 32 P-40 fighters to Java.

Australia was now under threat. On 19 February the carriers *Hiryu*, *Soryu*, *Akagi* and *Kaga* launched a strike force of 188 aircraft against Darwin, the only major port in northern Australia. It was from here that the crumbling defence of Java was being supplied and it also provided a base from which to challenge the bulging line of Japanese conquest to the south.

The defence was overwhelmed, fighter planes being once again caught on the ground. Ten US Army Air Force P-40s under the command of Major F.S. Pell, returning to Darwin after an unsuccessful attempt to reach Timor, intercepted. One P-40 shot down an attacker before being promptly shot down itself. A second wave of high-level bombers attacked the airfield before any more defenders could get airborne. Val dive-bombers struck the harbour, sinking transports loaded with fuel and ammunition and a destroyer, the USS *Peary*, for the loss of only two aircraft.

The end in Java itself came quickly. By 28 February the total strength of fighters left was less than a squadron, but the hopeless fight continued. The pilots and ground staff of No 232 Squadron RAF

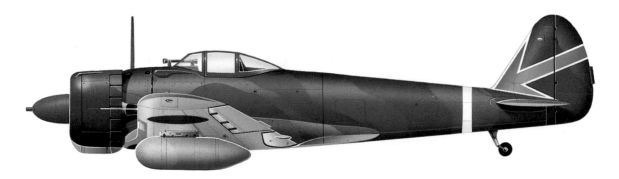

A Nakajima Ki-43-1c of HQ Chutai, based in northern Thailand, in early 1942.

volunteered to fight on. On 1 March the squadron, supported by ten Dutch P-40s and ten Dutch Buffaloes, attacked the Japanese beachhead at Evatan-wetan.

Burma and the Indian Ocean

At the same time as Japanese forces were spreading out into the Southern Resources Area, the Japanese 15th Army was quietly marching westwards, unopposed, into Thailand. On 23 December the airbase at Victoria Point, on the southernmost tip of the British colony of Burma, was seized, effectively cutting air links from India to Malaya. On 19 January, with the conquest of Malaya looking secure, the invasion of Burma proper began, the capture of the capital, Rangoon, being its primary objective.

The element of surprise and the concentration of forces on the ground enabled the Japanese to push the defenders back very rapidly but, again, air power was of vital importance. From the opening of the campaign, bomber raids were launched against Rangoon but the Japanese Army Air Force met exceptionally stiff resistance from the pilots of Colonel Claire Chennault's American Volunteer Group (AVG), known as the 'Flying Tigers.'

On the outbreak of the Pacific War Chennault had sent one of his three squadrons of P-40 fighters (with their famous shark's teeth insignia) to Kunming in Yunnan Province in order to protect the Chinese end of the Burma Road, along which lend-lease supplies reached the embattled Chinese Nationalists.

The British asked for a second squadron to be sent to Mingaladon air base near Rangoon in order to strengthen the capital's feeble air defences. The third squadron was kept as a strategic reserve to reinforce the others and replace them in the line. The Kunming squadron's first action came on 20 December when Japanese bombers flying from Indochina were intercepted. Six Nakajima Ki-27s were shot down with no losses to the AVG. On the 23rd

Rangoon was raided, the AVG and RAF getting off the ground late but still managing to beat off the attackers at slight loss to themselves.

During January and February 1942 the Japanese Army Air Force intensified its attacks on Rangoon, strengthening the fighter escorts with reinforcements drawn from Malaya. The AVG pilots put up a magnificent resistance, shooting down over 100 Japanese aircraft for the loss of only 15 defenders. The Flying Tigers and the dwindling number of RAF aircraft operating from Mingaladon also flew ground-support missions for the hard-pressed British and Indian forces, who were falling back before the victorious Japanese 15th Army.

In the air the Japanese had taken a mauling but on the ground the battle was being lost, with scattered and demoralized forces unable to stop the Japanese onslaught. By 1 March, with Rangoon directly threatened, the escape routes were closing. Three jungle-weary Buffaloes, four P-40s and 30 Hurricanes of the RAF abandoned Mingaladon airfield, strewn with wrecked aircraft, and flew north to an airstrip carved out of paddy fields at Zigon. Chennault took his aircraft to the RAF base of Magwe in central Burma. From here RAF bombers launched a few ineffective raids against enemy air-bases in Thailand, and for three weeks the Allied air forces continued to support the battered British, Indian and Chinese armies in Burma.

On 21 March a massive Japanese air strike against Magwe, involving 230 aircraft caught the survivors on the ground. Chennault salvaged just three aircraft from the wreckage and withdrew to Loiwing just over the Chinese border. Eleven RAF Hurricanes and six Blenheims flew to Akyab on the coast, which was itself hit on the 27th – virtually wiping out the RAF in Burma. Some 20 officers and 324 airmen escaped in trucks overland to China, bearing with them a single radar set rescued from Magwe.

Rangoon fell on 7 March. At the end of a further

A Hawker Hurricane of 30 Squadron, RAF, Ceylon, 1942. The Hurricane was numerically the most important British aircraft in the Pacific war.

A Curtiss Warhawk of the American Volunteer Group in China in February 1942.

eight weeks the British were completely evicted from Burma, pushed back to the Indian frontier. This stunning victory, combined with the virtual obliteration of Allied naval power in the western Pacific, presented the Japanese Navy with a further colossal strategic opportunity – the securing of sea control in the Indian Ocean. This would throw a noose round India and effectively threaten the British position in the Middle East, where German and Japanese forces might even link up in a huge, hemispherical pincer movement.

On 15 March 1942 Admiral Nagumo, having cleared southern Java, led a powerful striking force of five carriers – the *Akagi*, *Soryu*, *Hiryu*, *Shokaku* and *Zuikaku*, together with four fast battleships – into the Indian Ocean, with the intention of destroying the British naval base of Colombo on the island of Ceylon (now Sri Lanka) and of catching Admiral Somerville's rebuilt Far Eastern force at anchor, in a replay of Pearl Harbor. A second Japanese force under Vice-Admiral Azawa, aboard *Ryujo*, was raiding in the Bay of Bengal.

After the debacle of Force Z the Royal Navy had managed to put together a new Far Eastern fleet, built around the veteran battleship *Warspite*, four even older World War I vintage battleships, together with the carriers *Indomitable* and *Formidable*, and the smaller carrier *Hermes*, plus eight cruisers and 15 destroyers.

Warned of Nagumo's foray, Somerville left Colombo, sailing southeast to meet the enemy, but the two fleets passed without making contact. Somerville turned back to the improvised base at Addu Atoll in the Maldives in order to refuel. The plan was now changed. Wary of Nagumo's preponderance in air power, and reluctant to seek a battle on the open ocean, Somerville despatched the vulnerable old battleships towards Africa out of harm's way, intending to use the carriers to launch a harrying night torpedo attack.

Nagumo pre-empted him. On Easter Sunday, 5 April 1942, 315 Japanese Navy aircraft bombed the ports of Colombo and Trincomalee but, although severe damage was done to repair facilities and oil storage sites, the harbours were largely empty of warships which had hurriedly evacuated the base. This time there was some effective fighter resistance led by Fleet Air Arm Fulmars and Sea Hurricanes flown ashore from HMS *Hermes*, and seven of the attackers were shot down.

However, the cruisers *Cornwall* and *Dorsetshire* were caught outside Colombo by 80 Navy dive-bombers in a force led by Lt-Commander Takashiye Egusa, air group commander of the *Soryu* and both ships were sunk within 19 minutes. A more critical loss was the carrier *Hermes*, rushed out to sea without her air group. She was caught by dive-bombers in the Bay of Bengal and quickly despatched.

It was enough. On 8 April, having demonstrated that Japan could control the Indian Ocean at will, Nagumo turned his carriers round and headed back through the Malacca Straits to Japan's new naval base at Singapore. In four months the 1st Air Fleet had operated across one-third of the globe and had sunk one carrier, five battleships, two cruisers and seven destroyers, and had damaged many more warships and shore installations without a single one of its own vessels being damaged.

US Raids

The shock caused by the Japanese onslaught was overwhelming. Long derided as little yellow men, whose industries could only slavishly copy the products of Birmingham or Pittsburgh, the soldiers, sailors and aircrew of the emperor suddenly assumed the role of supermen. Their aircraft appeared immune to attack and capable of the impossible. How could the Navy's G4M1 Betty bombers fly so far? How could single-engined Zero fighters span such long ranges over open ocean and outfly and outshoot any opposition?

Continued on page 55

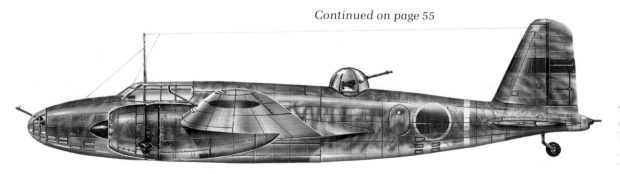

The Mitsubishi Ki-21, considered the best heavy bomber in Japanese service during World War II.

A Curtiss Warhawk with Chinese markings flown by 3rd Squadron of the American Volunteer Group, based at Kunming in China.

Japanese Navy Mitsubishi G3M 'Nell' bombers set out to attack the Burmese capital Rangoon.

The North American
B-25 Mitchell. The
first production
machine was flown in
August 1940.

Keith Fretwell

Top. A specially lightened B-25 Mitchell prepares for take-off from the carrier *Hornet*. *Left.* A B-25 lumbers off the flight-deck to take part in the attack on Japanese cities in April 1942.

A Boeing B-17 Flying Fortress belonging to 14th Squadron, based at Luzon, Philippines, in December 1941.

Below. Lt-General Jimmy Doolittle and Admiral Marc Mitscher aboard the USS *Hornet* preparing to launch the historic B-25 raid on Tokyo in April 1942.

An immediate priority for the US Navy was to take the war back to the enemy and at least dent his reputation for invincibility. Admiral Ernest J. King, the new chief of naval operations in Washington, demanded a 'defensive-offensive strategy.' However, the loss of the US Pacific fleet's battleships at Pearl ruled out an immediate counter-offensive. The lucky escape of the three carriers, *Lexington*, *Saratoga* and *Enterprise*, had, nevertheless, left intact the instrument by which the Japanese would eventually be rolled back — naval air power. On 11 January the *Saratoga* was severely damaged by a submarine-launched torpedo but the *Yorktown* arrived from the Atlantic soon afterwards. King ordered the new commander of the Pacific fleet, Admiral Chester W. Nimitz, to use the carriers to 'hit the Japanese where you can', while American air and naval strength in the Pacific was being rebuilt.

On 1 February 1942, therefore, the carriers *Enterprise* and *Yorktown*, commanded by Admiral William F. Halsey, launched air attacks on Japanese outposts in the Gilbert Islands and raided Kwajalein in the Marshalls, sinking a number of transports. Halsey's task force sortied from Pearl Harbor again to hit Wake island on 24 February and Marcus island on 4 March.

On 20 February a task force built around the *Lexington*, commanded by Vice-Admiral Wilson Brown, approached the newly seized Japanese base of Rabaul on the island of New Britain, by way of the Solomon Sea, aiming to launch a surprise attack. But, before they could hit their objective, they were pounced upon by aircraft of the Japanese 25th Air Flotilla and the first air battle between aircraft of the US and Japanese Navies took place, within full view of the crew of the *Lexington* who yelled encouragement to the pilots from its flight deck. Lieutenant Edward H. O'Hare of VF-42, flying an F4F-3 from the *Lexington*, encountered a formation of G4M1 land-based bombers. He shot down five of them, thus becoming the Navy's first ace of the war.

These were, however, pinpricks at the periphery of Japanese power. In Washington meanwhile a plan was being hatched to take the war to the heart of Japan's empire — Tokyo itself. To come within range medium bombers of the US Army Air Force would have to take off from aircraft carriers. An Army Air Force test-pilot, Colonel James H. Doolittle, was put in charge of this extraordinary operation and judged it to be feasible. In a hastily improvised combined operation, the Air Force bombers were stripped of unnecessary equipment and tested on an airstrip at Eglin Field, Florida, mocked up as the *Hornet*'s flight deck. They could just about make the short take-off, but they could not land. Accordingly, a one-way mission was planned: 16 B-25B Mitchells would be launched from the carrier *Hornet*, 13 of which would fly the 800 miles to Tokyo. The other three would hit Nagoya, Osaka and Kobe, and then all 16 would fly on a further 300 miles to the safety of airfields in China.

On 18 April 1942 the Mitchells lumbered off the *Hornet*'s flight deck, Halsey ordering them into the air earlier than planned, in the belief that his ships had been spotted by Japanese reconnaissance.

In fact the raid was a complete surprise. Of the 80 aircrew involved all but nine survived. Three taken prisoner were executed by the Japanese. The damage inflicted was minor, but it outraged the Japanese high command that the home islands could be struck with apparent impunity. They resolved to push out the outer perimeter of conquest still further — with disastrous results.

The new Grumman
TBF Avenger began to
replace the Devastator
in US Navy torpedo
squadrons from spring
1942 onwards.

CHAPTER 4

CORAL SEA
AND
MIDWAY

HOLDING THE
JAPANESE TIDE

From the opening of their great offensive in December 1941 to the high tide of conquest in April 1942, the Japanese had seized their objectives in half the time and with far fewer losses in men, ships and aircraft than had been expected.

A debate was taking place in the Imperial General Headquarters about what to do next. The Naval General Staff, headed by Admiral Osami Nagano, advocated a thrust southwards against Australia. The Army, however, with major forces engaged in China and Burma, was concerned about the number of troops this would require. Nagano adopted a modified strategy of striking southwest and isolating Australia by capturing Port Moresby in New Guinea and Tulagi in the Solomons. Tulagi in turn would be a springboard for assaults on New Caledonia, Fiji and Samoa.

Yamamoto, commander-in-chief of the Combined Fleet, meanwhile warned of the dangers presented by the still intact US carrier fleet, already making itself felt by its aggressive raiding. He advocated luring it into action and destroying it in a final cataclysmic battle as a prelude to a negotiated peace. The Doolittle raid against Tokyo lent weight to Yamamoto's argument, but preparations for the Port Moresby-Tulagi thrust had gone too far to be abandoned. However, the Combined Fleet commander was given his head – and also backing for a separate offensive operation against US targets that would surely bring the American carriers to battle. Yamamoto planned to attack a dot on the map called Midway, a tiny atoll 1135 miles westnorthwest of Pearl Harbor and a vital forward airfield for the Americans if nothing else. An attack on the western Aleutian Islands in the northern Pacific would be further bait designed to bring the US Navy to battle.

Thus the stage was set for two battles in the spring and early summer of 1942 in which naval air power would predominate. The first carrier-to-carrier battle in history, fought out in the Coral Sea, checked the Japanese drive on Port Moresby and the Battle of

A Douglas TBD-1 Devastator belonging to VT-6 aboard the USS *Enterprise* in early 1942.

Midway itself – one of the most decisive battles in history – was won by naval air power alone.

The Battle of the Coral Sea

As the first step in the new plan, Yamamoto ordered Admiral Shigeyoshi Inouye, commanding at Rabaul, to lead the thrust into the southern Solomons and New Guinea. On 1 May the small carrier *Shoho* led a task force of warships escorting an assault force of troop transports towards Tulagi, which was occupied on the 3 May without opposition. The next day aircraft from the *Yorktown* – Douglas SBD Dauntlesses and TBD Devastator torpedo-bombers – showed up over the island looking for targets. Most of the larger Japanese ships had already gone but the *Yorktown*'s strike aircraft managed to dispose of a destroyer and five seaplanes.

Meanwhile a larger Japanese force was assembled at Rabaul with the aim of assaulting Port Moresby by sea. It was supported by a striking force built round the large carriers *Shokaku* and *Zuikaku*, commanded by Admiral Takagi, which was moving south from the central Pacific in order to enter the Coral Sea from the east. The Japanese forces were thus dangerously dispersed, but there was a much greater weakness to their plans – the Americans could now read their intentions. US codebreakers had deciphered the high-level command signals of the Japanese Navy. Thus Admiral Nimitz could boldly concentrate forces to block the Japanese thrust and he despatched Admiral Fletcher with a task force led by *Lexington* and *Yorktown*, with a small squadron of US and Australian cruisers, into the Coral Sea.

At the same time Takagi's powerful carrier force steamed into the sea from the northeast, just as the *Shoho* detachment (which had joined up with the Port Moresby ships) was approaching the area from the Solomon Sea in the north. At this stage, in spite of reconnaissance efforts, neither side was aware of the other's presence.

Then at 0815 on 7 May an American search aircraft reported the sighting of two carriers and four heavy cruisers. Admiral Fletcher ordered a strike and 93 aircraft were launched from *Lexington* and *Yorktown*, only to discover as they approached the target area that the report was wrong. There were no carriers – only two cruisers and two destroyers. Fletcher let the strike continue, a gamble rewarded when at 1100 the Dauntless pilots found the *Shoho* beneath them; 53 US aircraft attacked the ship, which was smothered by bomb hits and rocked by seven torpedo strikes. The light carrier was quickly ablaze and sinking. Lt-Commander Bob Dixon signalled *Lexington* the famous message 'Scratch one flattop, Dixon to carrier, scratch one flattop!'

The exposed Port Moresby invasion force turned

Below. The 'Lady Lex' blazes after taking multiple torpedo and bomb hits during the Battle of the Coral Sea.

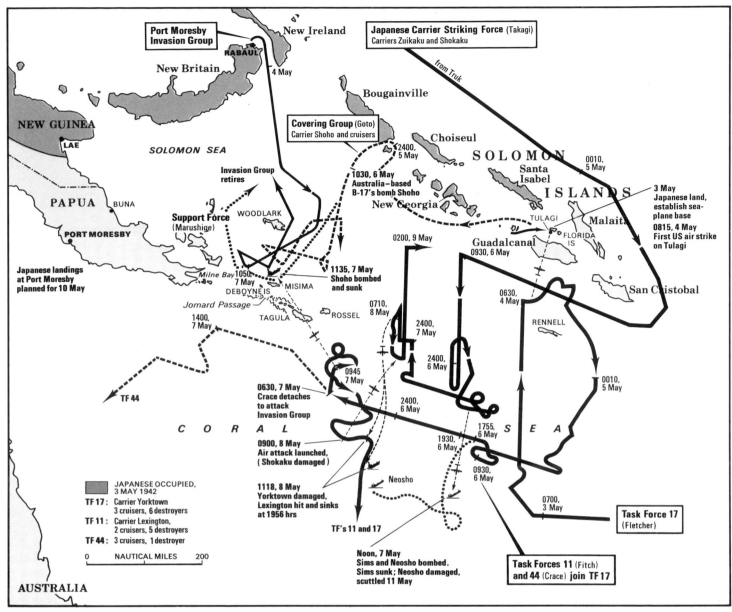

Port Moresby Invasion Group

Japanese Carrier Striking Force (Takagi)
Carriers Zuikaku and Shokaku

New Ireland

RABAUL
4 May

New Britain

from Truk

NEW GUINEA

LAE

SOLOMON SEA

Bougainville

Covering Group (Goto)
Carrier Shoho and cruisers

Choiseul

SOLOMON

0010,
5 May

2400,
5 May

1030, 6 May
Australia–based
B-17's bomb Shoho

ISLANDS

Santa
Isabel

PAPUA

BUNA

Invasion Group
retires

WOODLARK

New Georgia

TULAGI

Malaita

3 May
Japanese land,
establish sea-
plane base

0815, 4 May
First US air strike
on Tulagi

PORT MORESBY

Support Force
(Marushige)

0200, 9 May

FLORIDA
IS

Japanese landings
at Port Moresby
planned for 10 May

Milne Bay
1050,
7 May

1135, 7 May
Shoho bombed
and sunk

Guadalcanal
0930, 6 May

San Cristobal

DEBOYNE IS

MISIMA

Jomard Passage

TAGULA

ROSSEL

0710,
8 May

0630,
4 May

RENNELL

1400,
7 May

TF 44

0945
7 May

2400,
7 May

2400,
6 May

0010,
5 May

0630, 7 May
Crace detaches
to attack
Invasion Group

C O R A L

2400,
6 May

S E A

1755,
6 May

0900, 8 May
Air attack launched,
(Shokaku damaged)

1930,
6 May

0930,
6 May

0700,
3 May

1118, 8 May
Yorktown damaged,
Lexington hit and sinks
at 1956 hrs

Neosho

Task Force 17
(Fletcher)

JAPANESE OCCUPIED,
3 MAY 1942

TF 17: Carrier Yorktown
3 cruisers, 6 destroyers

TF 11: Carrier Lexington,
2 cruisers, 5 destroyers

TF 44: 3 cruisers, 1 destroyer

TF's 11 and 17

0   NAUTICAL MILES   200

Noon, 7 May
Sims and Neosho bombed.
Sims sunk; Neosho damaged,
scuttled 11 May

Task Forces 11 (Fitch)
and 44 (Crace) **join TF 17**

AUSTRALIA

Above. **The Battle of the Coral Sea.**

round for the safety of Rabaul, but aircraft from the *Shokaku* and *Zuikaku* were vengefully hunting for the US carriers. They thought they had found them when they sank a fleet oiler and a destroyer. Realizing their mistake, that evening aboard *Shokaku*, Admiral Takagi ordered another strike to be launched as darkness fell. Nine aircraft were shot down by US fighters flying offensive combat air patrols. In the darkness several Japanese pilots

mistook the US carriers for their own and one even tried to land on the *Yorktown*. Eleven crashed as they attempted to land in the dark on their own carriers. In all, 21 out of 26 aircraft failed to return safely.

Dawn on the next day, 8 May, found each side roughly equal in numbers of ships and aircraft available. From a range of 175 miles the Americans got their strike in first, when dive-bombers and

A Douglas SBD-3 Dauntless of VSB-6 aboard the USS Enterprise in early 1942.

torpedo-bombers from *Yorktown* attacked the *Sho-kaku*. Nine planes made torpedo runs but not a single torpedo functioned properly. The dive-bombers fared better, with two hits on the big carrier's flight deck. She could no longer operate aircraft but she was still afloat – to fight again another day. The *Zuikaku* meanwhile had disappeared into a rain squall but managed to get off a counter-strike. Japanese aircraft found the American carriers with their guard down – some of the 17 Wildcats of their protecting combat air patrol were on deck refuelling. The *Yorktown* managed to dodge eight torpedoes but was struck by Val dive-bombers. One bomb sliced through four decks, killing 66 crewmen.

Lexington was struck by several bombs and up to five torpedoes. Damage control measures kept her afloat and she began to slowly limp back to Pearl Harbor under her own steam. But several hours later, fumes from fractured aviation fuel lines ignited, sending a fireball through the ship's insides and blasting aircraft clean off her flight deck. At 1710 Captain Frederick C. Sherman gave the order to abandon ship. Most of the 3000-man crew were taken off before the blazing hulk was sunk by five torpedoes from the escorting destroyer USS *Phelps*.

Coral Sea was the first great aircraft carrier battle; no surface ship on either side sighted the enemy. Tactically it could be counted a draw – the Americans lost more ships, the Japanese lost more aircraft (97 to the US total of 77) – but the Japanese strategic objective, the thrust on Port Moresby, had been thwarted. The damaged *Yorktown* was soon back in

Admiral Chester Nimitz, commander-in-chief of the Pacific Fleet from 31 December 1941.

Below. USS *Lexington's* Grumman F4F Wildcat fighters spotted on deck during the Battle of the Coral Sea.

The Japanese carrier *Hiryu* manoeuvres at high speed to successfully evade bombs dropped by US Army Air Force B-17s from a high level, 4 June 1942.

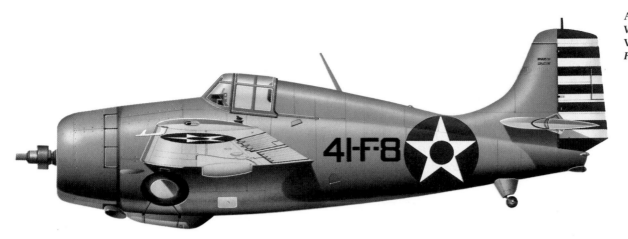

A Grumman F4F-4
Wildcat belonging to
VF-41 aboard the USS
Ranger early in 1942.

action but the *Shokaku* would require long months of repair and the unscathed *Zuikaku*'s air groups had been badly mauled. Neither carrier would be available for the next great stage of the recast Japanese plans – the thrust west to Midway, and to the northwest (in a diversionary attack on the Aleutians) in an attempt to bring the US carrier fleet to a final battle of annihilation.

The Battle of Midway
This grand objective was to be achieved by a very

powerful striking force – 165 warships in all, virtually the total naval strength of the Japanese Empire. At its cutting edge were four fleet and two light aircraft carriers, seven battleships, and 13 cruisers and destroyers. Convinced that both *Yorktown* and *Lexington* had been sunk in the Coral Sea actions, the Combined Fleet commander, Admiral Yamamoto, planned an audacious division of force with multiple objectives and diversionary targets in order to wrong-foot the Americans. The fleet was divided as follows.

Below. TBD
Devastator torpedo-
bombers of VT-6
aboard USS
Enterprise prepare for
their disastrous strike
against the Japanese
fleet at Midway. Only
four of the aircraft
shown in this
photograph returned.

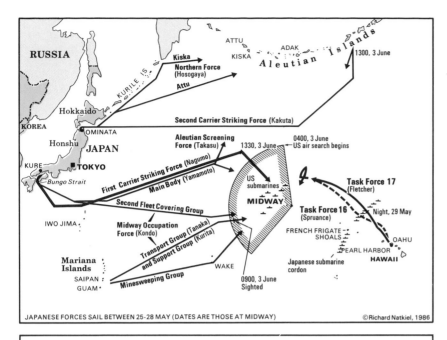

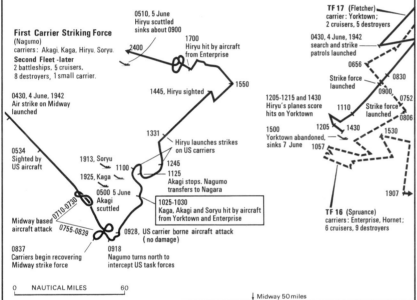

Above. **The Battle of Midway.**

and Kiska were to be directly seized.

- The First Carrier Striking Force, under Admiral Nagumo, with the carriers *Soryu, Kaga, Akagi* and *Hiryu*. Nagumo's task was straightforward. He was to hit Midway at dawn on 4 June and knock out its air defences. He would then proceed to soften it up for the amphibious assault that would go in later in the day. After that he was to engage the US Pacific fleet, which would surely try to intervene.

- The Midway Occupation Force of troop transports protected by a powerful screening force of two battleships, a light carrier and seven cruisers. This force was to put 51,000 troops ashore on Midway beginning at dusk on 5 June.

- The Main Body comprising seven battleships – including the mighty *Yamato*, the largest warship afloat, serving as Yamamoto's own flagship. Positioned 300 miles west of Nagumo's carriers, the Combined Fleet Commander planned to use the battleships to move in and crush any survivors once Nagumo had mauled the Pacific fleet.

Dividing the force in this manner and committing it to a precisely time-tabled schedule depended on surprise (and thus on complete secrecy) and the absence of the US carriers from the Midway area until at least 8 June. By this time the landings would have gone ahead and the island would have been secured. It also depended on an accurate fixing of the US carriers' position.

On 18 May a flying boat on patrol spotted US warships to the east of the Solomons; in fact, this was to be the last definite fix. The Japanese assumed, correctly, that they had retired to Pearl Harbor. In order to confirm this a long-range reconnaissance mission was launched from a base in the Marshall Islands, using an Emily flying boat. This was scheduled to refuel from a submarine at French Frigate Shoals, then arrive over Hawaii on the night of 30 May. The plan was aborted when it was discovered that a US Navy seaplane detachment was already using the shoals. Japanese submarines arrived at the northern and southern ends of the Hawaiian archipelago on 3 June, too late to catch and stalk the two US task forces (Task Force 16, *Enterprise* and *Hornet*, with cruiser and destroyer escorts, and Task Force 17, built around the *Yorktown*, which left Pearl on 28 May and 30 May respectively). The two fleets met at 'Point Luck', 325 miles northeast of Midway atoll, on the evening on 2 June, waiting for

- The Northern Area Force, commanded by Admiral Boshiro Hosogaya, which was allotted the two light carriers, *Ryujo* and *Junyo*, from which diversionary air attacks on bases in the Aleutians would be launched. After that the islands of Attu

Continued on page 66

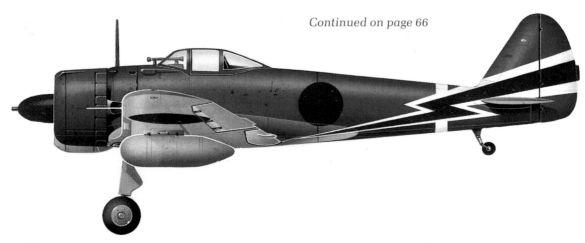

A Nakajima Ki-43-1c Hayabusa, a variant of the 1a, was widely used in the Pacific war.

The Douglas SBD
Dauntless, variously
known by its crews as
the 'Barge' or the
'Speedy-D', proved the
instrument of victory
at Midway.

the next indication of the enemy's movements.

In contrast to Japanese supposition and guess-work, Admiral Nimitz could read the enemy's intentions much more accurately, courtesy of his codebreakers. By mid-May he knew enough to strengthen Midway's defences considerably. The beaches around Eastern Island, where the vital airstrip was located, were heavily mined and wired. The Marine Corps garrison was reinforced to over 2000 men – and the air defences were augmented. Until now there had been only 21 Brewster Buffalo fighters and 16 Vought Vindicator dive-bombers on strength. During the last week of May, 18 Marine SBDs, seven F4F Wildcats, six brand-new Navy TBF Avenger torpedo-bombers and four twin-engined Army Air Force B–26 Marauder medium bombers equipped to carry torpedoes were flown in. Reconnaissance was stepped up, with 32 PBY Catalinas (now based on the island) flying standing patrols in a huge arc southwest to northeast out to a range of 700–800 miles. A further 18 B–17s shuttled in on a daily round flight from Oahu to Midway. On 30 May they were switched to search and attack missions to westward – in the likely area of any Japanese approach.

Midway's land-based air power was thus going to be an important factor, but Nimitz realized that, even though they had been forewarned by intelligence of the Japanese diversionary tactics, the fate of the island and its garrison would depend on naval support – and in particular air support from the carriers. He could muster only three – the *Enterprise* and the *Hornet* recalled from patrol in the south Pacific plus, amazingly, the *Yorktown*, made combat-ready in a 48-hour period at Pearl Harbor after her mauling in the Coral Sea. Three of her boilers were still out of action, reducing her speed. The three carriers could carry approximately 250 aircraft, about the same as Nagumo's 1st Air Fleet, which would spearhead the assault on Midway itself.

Admiral Halsey, meanwhile, had been taken ill with a skin rash and was hospitalized. He was replaced as commander of Task Force 16 (*Enterprise* and *Hornet*) by the quieter, more methodical Raymond A. Spruance. The latter was not one of the more colourful naval commanders, but was to provide badly needed cool judgment in the testing days to come. Admiral Fletcher, directing Task Force 17 from the *Yorktown*, was in command at sea, under Nimitz's direct authority at Pacific Fleet

Above. A Grumman TBF Avenger, one of the US Navy's leading aircraft in the Pacific war.

Opposite. Lieutenant Edward 'Butch' O'Hare, VF-3 Squadron's Wildcat ace. O'Hare shot down five Japanese aircraft single-handed in an air battle at Bougainville in February 1942 – he was killed in action in November 1943. Chicago International airport is named after him.

Headquarters, Pearl Harbor.

Both sides made their opening thrusts on 3 June. At first light, in the northern Pacific, Japanese aircraft took off from Hosogaya's Northern Area Force carriers to attack Dutch Harbor in the Aleutians, making some very loud diversionary bangs as they hit the oil storage sites. Nimitz kept his nerve, waiting for the vital reconnaissance report that the expected main thrust across the central Pacific had been sighted. Shortly before 0900 a PBY radioed a sighting – a large body of ships some 700 miles out heading for Midway.

The American commanders deduced correctly that this was the slower-moving Midway Occupation Force. The first reaction was to get Midway's offensive long-range air power into the air. Nine B–17s took off at 1200 and ineffectually bombed the transports from a high altitude four hours later. That night four PBYs made an air-to-surface radar-directed attack in darkness but managed only to inflict slight damage on a tanker.

But where were the Japanese carriers? By dawn on 4 June Nagumo's First Carrier Striking Force was emerging from dense rain squalls but still shielded by broken cloud as it approached the launch point, 240 miles northwest of the target. Meanwhile Fletcher and Spruance were steaming in a southwesterly direction heading for a point which would put them some 200 miles north of Midway – within scouting range of Nagumo's force. At 0430 the *Yorktown* put ten SBDs up with orders to search a 100-mile arc to the north – empty ocean.

Some 250 miles away to the east, confident that there were no US carriers screening his approach, Nagumo launched the first wave of strike aircraft against Midway – 36 Nakajima B5N2 Kates from the *Hiryu* and *Soryu*, 36 Aichi D3A2 Vals from the *Akagi* and *Kaga*, together with 36 escorting Zeros, nine from each carrier. The Kates and Vals were armed with general-purpose demolition bombs for use against land targets. In charge of this force was Lt-Commander Joichi Tomonaga.

A lone Midway-based PBY spotted a Japanese seaplane heading towards the atoll. Following its course in the opposite direction, at 0534 the US Navy patrol bomber pilot spotted two of Nagumo's carriers and radioed their position, speed and course to Midway. Minutes later another PBY caught sight of Tomonaga's strike formation on their run-in, getting off the stark warning 'Many planes, heading Midway. Bearing 320°, distant 150 miles.'

Fletcher heard the report on the *Yorktown* and immediately recalled the SBDs futilely searching to the north. He ordered Spruance to turn away southwest and engage the enemy. He would follow as soon as the Dauntlesses were recovered. On Midway itself, on receipt of the warning all serviceable aircraft were scrambled – no-one was going to be caught on the ground this time.

The Midway aircraft had two priorities – to deflect the incoming attack and get through to strike at the carriers from which they were launched. Both attempts went badly wrong for the Americans. The defending F2A Buffaloes and F4F Wildcats met the

Above. An Aichi D3A2 'Val' dive-bomber; 126 D3As took part in the strike on Pearl Harbor. The type was equally triumphant in Nagumo's sweep through the Indian Ocean, but the aircraft and their élite crews suffered heavy losses at Coral Sea, Midway and around Guadalcanal.

Opposite. An Aichi D3A 'Val' makes its bomb run at Pearl Harbor.

attackers less than 30 miles out from their target, and were rapidly outgunned and outflown by the Zeros: 17 Marine Corps fighters were quickly shot down and seven more damaged. Meanwhile the Japanese carrier-launched B5N2 Kates and D3A2 Vals swept through the ragged defences, pounding targets on the island for 30 minutes, but leaving the airstrip intact for future use. Despite having caused considerable damage, the strike commander, Tomonaga, could see that Midway was still very much in business and radioed the 1st Air Fleet to call up a second attack.

Meanwhile, Nagumo was himself fending off attacks. Six TBF Avenger torpedo-bombers went in low, in the teeth of intense anti-aircraft fire, harried by Zeros as they wheeled into their bombing runs. Three TBFs were shot down before they could even launch their torpedoes. Two more were shot out of the air and only one got back to Midway — severely damaged. One Japanese officer later recalled that the American torpedoes 'didn't have any speed at all' and one was blown up by machine-gun fire as it moved fitfully through the water. The Army Air Force B−26s came in next, releasing their torpedoes at 800 yards, but they were easily evaded by the carriers. Two of the medium bombers were shot down, one nearly hitting the *Akagi* before plunging into the sea on fire.

On the bridge of his flagship Nagumo had to think quickly. In spite of the apparent ease in deflecting these attacks, it seemed imperative that Midway's air defences should be crushed before the assault ships arrived. Where were the US carriers? Surely they could not intervene now. The admiral took the fateful decision to rearm all available aircraft with blast bombs in order to attack targets on the ground at Midway.

Before despatching the first strike wave against the atoll, Nagumo had launched seven long-range scout aircraft, including two seaplanes each from the cruisers *Tone* and *Chikuma*. Their task was to fly in a broad arc to the east of Midway, and to search and report in case any US naval units should indeed be in the area. An aircraft from *Chikuma* passed close to the US carriers at around 0630 but failed to spot them, nor did the pilot report the fact that he had encountered and engaged a scouting SBD from *Yorktown*, indicating the presence of a carrier. One of the *Tone*'s aircraft was delayed half an hour until 0550 by catapult trouble, a trivial incident at the time but one which was to have grave consequences. The admiral had kept in reserve an anti-warship strike force of torpedo- and dive-bombers, plus escorting Zeros armed and ready, scattered on the flight deck in case the elusive American carriers should show up. These were the aircraft which his artificers were now toiling to rearm, cranking the Kates down from the flight deck to be relieved of their torpedoes and loaded with blast bombs. This frenzy of activity was in progress when at 0728 the belatedly launched seaplane from the *Tone* radioed in an urgent sighting: 'Ten enemy surface warships in position bearing 10°, distance 240 miles from Midway, course 150°, speed over 20 knots.'

This was bad news but there were much more immediate problems: 16 SBDs from Midway made an attack, concentrating on the *Hiryu*. Ten bombs

A Brewster F2A-3
Buffalo belonging to
VMF-221, stationed at
Hawaii in mid-1942.

were dropped, all missed and only half the force escaped the attentions of the defending Zeros. A group of B–17s now made a high-level attack on the *Hiryu* and *Soryu*, again without effect, and an attack by a squadron of Vought SB2U Vindicators was easily beaten off. However, much more urgent threat was lurking over the horizon. At 0820 came a message from the distant reconnaissance seaplane that the enemy force appeared to include an aircraft carrier.

The Midway attack plan depended on critical timing – not simply for the effecting of the strategic junction of the Combined Fleet's divided forces but for Nagumo's attack waves to be launched and retrieved in a precisely choreographed order. The presence of enemy carriers was revealed at the critical moment when the 1st Air Fleet had completed rearming for a land-attack mission and the fighter reserves had been used up fending off the counter-strikes from Midway (many of the Zeros had

A Dauntless leads five
TBD Devastators
down USS
Enterprise's flight
deck, April 1942.

Above. **A Landing Signals Officer on board CV-7 in June 1942.**

run out of fuel). Moreover, from 0830 onwards Tomonaga's aircraft began returning from the initial strike, low on fuel, some of them damaged.

Nagumo ordered the second strike to be delayed, all aircraft on deck to be struck below, so that the returning first wave could be recovered. By 0915 recovery was complete and the sweating deck crews worked frantically to refuel and rearm all available aircraft with torpedoes and armour-piercing bombs. At 0918 the Japanese ships made a 90 degree change of course to east-north-east, Nagumo now intending to launch the second strike at 1030.

When news of the attack on Midway reached Spruance commanding Task Force 16, he decided to launch a full-scale strike from both his carriers, *Enterprise* and *Hornet*, as quickly as possible. Timing was crucial – the two fleets were now approximately 155 miles apart. The combat radius of the American aircraft was 175 miles, a distance they could cover in little under an hour. There would be slight room for error and little time over the target. The admiral's chief-of-staff, Captain Miles Browning, calculated that the best moment for a strike was imminent – the Japanese carriers would be busy recovering the aircraft that had struck Midway and at their most vulnerable.

Meanwhile in their ready rooms aboard the *Hornet* and *Enterprise*, US Navy pilots waited for the order 'pilots man your planes', joking bravely as the tension rose. The briefing was simple enough – it would be a full-scale strike, leaving only a few fighters behind for self defence. The *Enterprise*'s Air Group, commanded by Lt-Commander Clarence McClusky would launch 33 SBD Dauntlesses of squadrons VB-6 (bombing) and VS-6 (scouting), 14 TBD Devastators of VT-6 (torpedo) and ten F4F Wildcats from VF-6 (fighting).

The *Hornet*'s Air Group, led by Lt-Commander Stanhope Ring, would launch 35 SBDs from VB-8 and VS-8, 15 Devastators from VT-8 and ten F4Fs from VF-8. The co-ordinated launch was scheduled to take an hour. The first aircraft up would circle over the carriers until the last aircraft, the TBDs were got into the air but at 0745, knowing he had been sighted by the Japanese reconnaissance seaplane from the *Tone*, Spruance gave McClusky and Ring the order to get their air groups up. All squadrons were airborne by 0806, but the precision of the formation had been broken in the hurry to launch.

The F4Fs of Squadron VF-6 from *Enterprise*, detailed to cover the TBDs of Squadron VT-6 (led by Lt-Commander Eugene Lindsey), in fact took station on the TBDs of Squadron VT-8, (led by Lt-Commander John Waldron), part of the *Hornet*'s air group. The strike force from the two carriers flew off towards the target area in four loose groups – the SBDs from *Enterprise*, the SBDs and F4Fs from *Hornet*, the TBDs from *Hornet* protected by VF-6, the F4Fs from the *Enterprise* and, finally, *Enterprise*'s unescorted VT-6, Lindsey's TBD Devastators.

At 0838 Admiral Fletcher began launching *Yorktown*'s Air Group – 17 TBDs of VB-3 (led by Lt-Commander Maxwell Leslie), 12 Devastators of VT-3 (led by Lt-Commander Lance Massey) and six F4Fs of VF-3 (led by Lt-Commander John Thach). All were airborne by 0906 hours.

As the two Air Groups flew towards the target area, Nagumo had meanwhile changed direction. The aircraft from *Enterprise* and *Hornet* overshot the new Japanese course, searching fruitlessly to the southeast above the haze. Some of the F4Fs ran out of fuel and had to ditch in the ocean. The longer-range SBDs headed back to the *Hornet*. Some made their way to Midway airstrip, where three crashed on landing. The Devastators of VT-8 meanwhile had steered a more westerly course, losing their fighter escort in the cloud cover in the process. At around 0920 Waldron's group sighted the enemy ships and began their attack, running low and slow into a wall of anti-aircraft fire. Without their fighter escorts, the Devastators were slaughtered. They were met, still miles out from their target, by defending Zeros which danced around the lumbering TBDs, riddling them with cannon and machine-gun fire. All 15 of Waldron's squadron were shot down in flames without scoring a hit. One man survived, Ensign George H. Gay, to be picked out of the sea the next day by a PBY.

VT-6, which had lost its fighter cover in the launch, arrived 15 minutes later. Lindsey's squadron attacked the *Kaga* from both sides but, as the TBDs wheeled in to make their beam attacks, the Zeros struck again. No torpedoes hit the target and ten TBDs, including the commander's, were shot down.

Yorktown's torpedo squadron appeared at approximately 1000, having also lost its fighter cover on the way. It was another massacre as VT-3's aircraft tried to get into launch positions to hit the *Soryu*, only to be swatted into the sea by Zeros. Ten aircraft were lost in this last torpedo attack. In three assaults not a single hit had been made on an enemy warship, but 35 American aircraft had been lost.

The SBD dive-bombers of VB-6 and VS-6 had also been thwarted by Nagumo's change of course and were running low on fuel. Lt-Commander Clarence McClusky made a fateful decision when he decided to search to the northwest rather than to the southeast. At 0955 he spotted the destroyer *Arashi*, which had been depth-charging an American submarine. The formation followed it, spotting the main fleet at 1005 through a break in the clouds.

Nagumo's carriers were steaming in a diamond formation, his flagship, the *Akagi*, to the west, the *Soryu* on her starboard beam, the *Kaga* astern and the *Hiryu*, commanded by Rear Admiral Yamaguchi away to the north surrounded by protecting battleships, cruisers and destroyers. McClusky went straight in for the *Kaga*, while five SBDs from VB-6 bore down on the *Akagi*.

The Douglas SBD Dauntless, variously known to its crews as the 'Barge' or the 'Speedy D', was not the most modern warplane when it first saw combat but its outstanding feature was its ability to provide a rock-solid platform in a steep dive, so that the pilot could release his bombs accurately. Dive angles varied, although 80 degrees was considered the

SBD Dauntlesses flying over a Japanese carrier during the Battle of Midway.

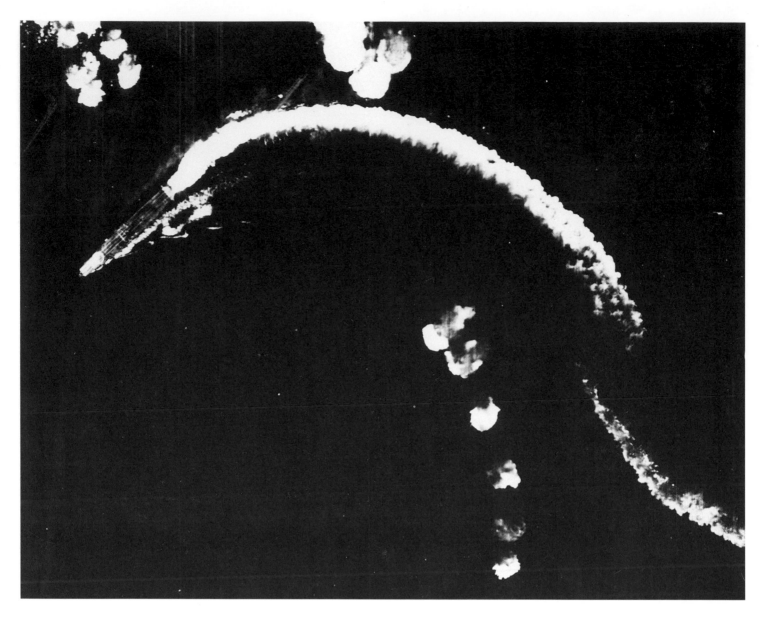

optimum. Although draughty and noisy and notoriously tiring to fly in long over-water flights, the machine was forgiving in battle when the best altitude or airspeed at the roll-in point, as a dive began, were not easy to achieve.

Many pilots learned to make quick corrections while plummeting seawards and to master the art of pulling out while at the same time taking evasive action to throw off enemy gunners. The SBD's airframe was built to take high stress and pilots could throw it around aggressively, pulling up to nine-g without breaking the machine apart.

US Navy doctrine made good use of the SBD's attributes. The standard attack formation was 18 aircraft strong, flying stacked up towards the sun in three groups of six aircraft each, flying in three-ship V-formations.

From an altitude of 15,000 feet the squadron leader, flying up-sun at the top of the stack, would initiate the attack, peeling off and diving, being followed in sequence by the entire formation. To begin a dive SBD pilots would first throttle back, lifting the aircraft's nose to force the beginning of a stall. Operating a lever to his right, the pilot now activated the landing flaps and dive brakes, pulling

the aircraft over on its side to fly 'down the chute', the dive brakes holding the speed to around 275 mph.

The dive to the release altitude of between 2000 and 1500 feet took 30 nerve-racking seconds, during which time the pilot had to line up the target through his sight and try to compute aim-off for target speed and wind direction, while continuing to fly his aircraft with light touches on the stick and rudder.

The crutch gear was released, cradling the 1000-lb bomb and swinging it clear of the propeller arc. With target bore-sighted the pilot had to pull the manual bomb release lever, sending 1000 lbs of high explosive plunging towards the target.

After bomb release the pilot now had to open the throttle to maximum and pull the stick hard back. With dive brakes retracted the SBD would sharply accelerate while reversing its angle. The pilot often had to press the arteries in his neck with his left hand as he pulled the stick back with his right, in order to prevent blood draining backwards and a subsequent blackout, as he attempted at the same time to throw his aircraft into an evasive manoeuvre.

The first SBD-launched bomb hit Nagumo's flagship *Akagi* amidships, detonating the bombs still

Above. **The Japanese carrier *Zuikaku* at the Battle of the Coral Sea, manoeuvring hard to dodge torpedo attacks, 8 May 1942.**

littering the hangar deck in a series of explosion which surged upwards, ripping the flight deck open. A second bomb hit aircraft parked on the rear flight deck, starting fires which swept through the carrier. By 1047 she was abandoned, Nagumo transferring his flag to the cruiser *Nagara*. Four more SBD-delivered bombs ripped through the *Kaga* starting a chain of explosions and fires.

Meanwhile, unknown to McClusky, the dive-bombers of *Yorktown*'s VB-3 had arrived, led by one of the US Navy's most experienced aviators, Lt-Commander Maxwell Leslie. At 1025 13 of his aircraft began their dive from 14,500 feet, plunging on the *Soryu* in three waves. The Japanese carrier was hit three times near the forward and midship aircraft lifts, wrecking the flight deck and spreading explosions and fire among parked aircraft, and fuel and bomb storage compartments. She was ablaze from end to end within 20 minutes.

Admiral Yamaguchi aboard *Hiryu*, standing off to the north, saw three oily blooms of smoke on the southern horizon and ordered an immediate strike. By 1058 18 dive-bombers and six fighters were in the air led by Lieutenant Michio Kobayashi, who had no precise information on the position of his American opponents.

The attackers spotted aircraft of VB-3 scurrying home to the *Yorktown* after the attack on *Soryu* and followed them. Around noon the *Yorktown*'s radar picked up Kobayashi's flight at a range of 40 miles. F4F Wildcats were hastily launched and fighters from the *Enterprise* and *Hornet* flew in to put 28 F4Fs in the air above the target carrier as Leslie's returning SBDs were warned off out of the danger area.

The defence of the *Yorktown* by the fighter planes and by the anti-aircraft gunners on the screen of escorting cruisers and destroyers around her was determined, but eight Vals got through, striking the carrier with three bombs. One hit the flight deck, the second exploded near the forward magazines and the third went straight down the smokestack, putting out the furnace fires of five of the six boilers. The *Yorktown* was still afloat, but capable of only six knots and her communications had been wrecked. At 1315 Admiral Fletcher transferred his flag to the cruiser *Astoria* and some of the *Yorktown*'s aircraft took refuge on the *Hornet* and *Enterprise*. Damage control parties, meanwhile, had managed to patch the flight deck and relight four boilers, getting the speed up to 20 knots.

Admiral Yamaguchi now received a report from a reconnaissance flight, launched earlier by the *Soryu*, that he was facing three American carriers, and another strike was readied. Ten Kate torpedo-bombers and six Zeros took off. Soon they found a seemingly undamaged US carrier and again the pilots flew unhesitatingly through a wall of anti-aircraft fire. Five Kates were shot down on their torpedo runs but four more managed to launch from close range. Two torpedoes struck the warship amidships ripping open her double-bottom fuel tanks. Water poured in and within 20 minutes the huge carrier was listing at an angle of 26 degrees.

In fact the *Hiryu*'s aircraft had found the *Yorktown* for a second time. The survivors of the Japanese strike force, five Kates and three Zeros, got back to the *Hiryu* at 1630 to claim one US carrier severely damaged. Knowing that the earlier dive bomber strike had left *Yorktown* dead in the water, Yamaguchi assumed that his strike had crippled a second carrier, not realizing that the *Yorktown* had in fact been attacked twice. He judged that each side now had one carrier intact – by no means impossible odds for continuing the action.

There were few strike aircraft left on *Hiryu*, but this handful were prepared for a final attack to be launched at 1800 that evening. It was not to be. *Enterprise* and *Hornet* were very much intact and at 1530 and 1603 hours each carrier launched 23 and 16 SBDs respectively, with the *Hiryu* as their target. Without radar the Japanese did not see them coming. The *Enterprise*'s aircraft (including ten refugees from *Yorktown*) attacked at 1700, scoring four bomb hits in quick succession for the loss of three aircraft. Like her three sister ships the *Hiryu* was rapidly engulfed by fires and explosions, and by the time the *Hornet*'s aircraft appeared over the target at 1750, there was nothing left to attack – just a blazing hulk.

Throughout the night the four Japanese carriers burned. The *Soryu* blew up and finally sank at 0715 the next day, 5 June, followed 13 minutes later by the *Kaga*. Both the *Akagi* and *Hiryu* were scuttled by Japanese destroyers at dawn, although the *Hiryu* took four hours to sink, Admiral Yamaguchi going down with his ship. The crippled *Yorktown* had remained afloat and was being towed slowly back to Pearl Harbor when she and her accompanying destroyer were sunk by a torpedo from the Japanese submarine, I-168. These were the only US warship losses in a battle in which the Japanese had planned to destroy the US carrier fleet. Through the skill and bravery of US Navy pilots, aided by a fair amount of luck, the outcome of this victorious defensive battle was precisely the opposite of what had been intended. Four Japanese carriers went to the bottom along with 275 aircraft. US aircraft losses amounted to 132 – both land- and carrier-based. The Japanese tide of victories had been checked.

As a footnote to the Midway story the myth of Japanese invincibility was shattered in another way. For months Allied intelligence had been desperate to learn more about the Mitsubishi A6M Zero-Sen fighter – with its remarkable powers of manoeuvre and its almost mystical ability to turn up in completely unexpected places. One did precisely that – in the Aleutian Islands.

On 3 June Flight Petty Officer Tadayoshi Koga flew an almost brand-new Mitsubishi A6M2 Zero off the light carrier *Ryujo*, part of the Northern Area Force, his mission to escort bomber attacks on Dutch Harbor. On the return leg Koga discovered that his fuel tanks had been punctured by two bullets and he informed his flight commander of his intention to make an emergency landing.

Five weeks later a US Navy search party found the Zero upside down but virtually undamaged in a marsh on the island of Aktan. Koga was still at the controls, dead with a broken neck. The fighter was hurriedly shipped back to the United States where, restored to flying condition, it was exhaustively tested in order to expose its weaknesses.

CHAPTER 5

THE INVASION OF
THE SOLOMON ISLANDS

Guadalcanal

Above. **Grumman TBF Avengers. Their combat debut, with mixed success, was at Midway.**

Midway had stemmed the tide of Japanese conquest. Now, in the long series of air-sea-land battles for the island of Guadalcanal in the Eastern Solomons, that tide would be turned. To seize the island with its all-important airstrip, the first American offensive of the war was launched on 7 August 1942, when Major-General Alexander A. Vandengrift's 1st Marine Division landed on Guadalcanal and the much smaller islands of Gavutu and Tulagi.

With air cover provided by fighters flown from the *Saratoga, Enterprise* and *Wasp*, 16,000 men waded ashore to take the Japanese occupiers almost com-

pletely by surprise. It was just as well. By afternoon this early exercise in the amphibious warfare that the United States was later to excel in broke down in chaos as transports and supplies piled up on the beaches and incoming reinforcements wandered in vain looking for their correct rendezvous points. The move inland, with the capture of the half-completed Japanese airstrip as the primary objective, began to fall behind schedule.

On that first day the Japanese hit back from the air: 27 G4M bombers, escorted by 18 A6M Zeros, headed south from Rabaul in New Britain, 600 miles to the northwest, to hit the invasion fleet. Also scrambled were a flight of nine D3A1 Val dive-bombers, on a one-way mission, without the range to return to their

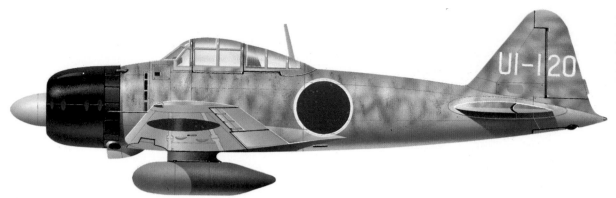

A Mitsubishi A6M3 'Zeke'. Popularly known as the Zero, it was the most famous Japanese fighter plane of World War II.

base. Two of the Japanese Navy's top fighter aces flew with the Zeros, Flight Officer Suburo Sakai and Warrant Officer Hiroyoshi Nishizawa. As they approached the island, the fighters split into two groups and Nishizawa's flight fell upon the Grumman F4Fs guarding the beaches. Five US aircraft were shot out of the air before Nishizawa broke off the fight. The G4M Betty bombers and Sakai's Zeros meanwhile swooped on the massed transports standing off the beaches but without scoring a single hit.

Wildcats from the carriers now engaged the bombers, shooting several down. Sakai destroyed a Wildcat in a savage, wheeling dogfight, the nimble Zero finally outflying and outshooting the tubby US Navy fighter.

Then the Zeros spotted another gaggle of US fighters. They attacked from astern, expecting a clean kill – only to be met by a blaze of fire from the rear machine-guns of the brand-new Grumman TBF torpedo-bombers. Sakai's Zero was riddled; he was blinded in one eye and received a serious head wound. The Japanese ace's aircraft began a seemingly final plunge into the sea but, revived by the stream of air through the shattered windscreen, Sakai managed to recover. Losing blood and suffering several blackouts, he nevertheless succeeded in nursing his battered fighter back to Rabaul.

The nine D3A Vals swooped vengefully on the invasion fleet. The destroyer *Mugford* was damaged by a bomb hit, but all the attacking aircraft were lost. Six were shot down and three fell into the sea, their tanks empty. In total, on that first day of the air fighting for Guadalcanal, the Japanese lost five G4Ms, six D3As, and two A6M Zeros, while the Americans lost eight Wildcats and an SBD Dauntless.

Late on the afternoon of 8 August the Marines were moving off the bridgehead, nosing inland to capture the airstrip already half scraped out of the

jungle, along with heavy construction equipment abandoned intact by the Japanese. That day the Japanese struck again from the air: 23 torpedo-armed G4M Bettys appeared over the invasion fleet, together with more D3A Vals and a Zero escort. A hail of anti-aircraft fire and dogged resistance by the Wildcat pilots brought down 18 of the attackers. The destroyer *Jarvis* was torpedoed but stayed afloat, and a transport was set on fire by a blazing Japanese aircraft whose pilot steered his doomed plane at the ship.

The air attacks were beaten off, but disaster awaited the US fleet. Outraged by this first serious assault on their conquests, Imperial General Headquarters ordered Lt-General Harukichi Hyakutate, commanding the 50,000 men of the 17th Army on Rabaul, to drive the Americans off Guadalcanal into the sea.

Meanwhile Vice-Admiral Gunichi Mikawa had put together a striking force of five heavy cruisers, two light cruisers and a destroyer and was racing from Rabaul. This force sailed impetuously through the 'Slot', the passage through the central Solomons, in daylight to hit the Allied ships off Savo Island in the early morning half-light of 9 August.

The Japanese force burst into Savo Sound at high speed to catch the invaders completely unprepared. They then sank four Allied cruisers and damaged another – all in the space of half an hour. The 'Long Lance' torpedo did most of the damage. This highly effective oxygen-fuelled weapon could travel over 11 miles at 49 knots.

Meanwhile, Admiral Fletcher had withdrawn his three carriers from the area for refuelling. But Mikawa was fearful of an air attack. Having scored a great victory against the cruiser force, he left the helpless transports alone and turned back to Rabaul.

The shock of Savo – the 'battle of the five sitting ducks' – and the withdrawal of the carriers left

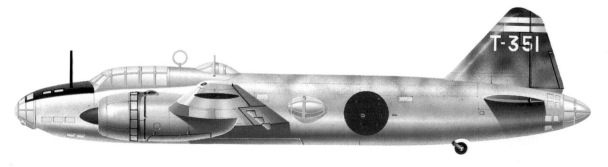

The Mitsubishi G4M land-based Japanese bomber proved vulnerable to Allied fighters and underwent considerable modifications.

Continued on page 82

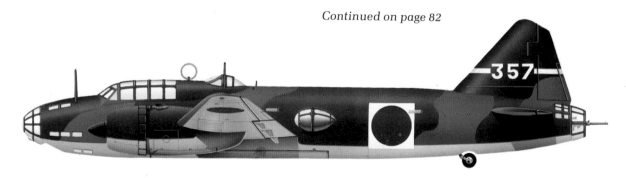

Above. **A captured Mitsubishi A6M Navy Type O carrier fighter on an evaluation flight in the United States.**

Admiral Richmond Kelly Turner, the commander of the amphibious force, little choice, but to pull back his ships in the face of an unquantified Japanese naval threat – with some Marines and most of the supplies still on board – leaving the main force ashore, in limbo, surrounded by enemy warships like sharks round a life-raft. The Japanese mounted day and night bombing raids while the Marine Seabees (construction battalions) ashore strove to complete the airstrip. It was named Henderson Field in honour of Major Lofton Henderson, a Marine SBD pilot lost at Midway. If US aircraft could be safely landed at Henderson, then the whole situation could be transformed.

The escort carrier *Long Island* brought in the first aircraft on 20 August. Two Marine Corps squadrons of Wildcats and SBDs were flown off the carrier to land at Henderson. Major John Smith, leader of the

fighter squadron, scored the first kill the next day, shooting down a Zero, the first of 19 kills he made during the campaign.

The jungle airstrip was now the strategic focus of a campaign that would grind on for months. Henderson Field would be the operating base for the pilots of the 'Cactus' air force (Cactus was the code name for the Guadalcanal-Tulagi area), an ad hoc formation where the niceties of squadron – even service – organization meant very little. The Marine air command echelon, the 1st Marine Air Wing, comprised all aircraft on the island, including Navy aircraft flown in to operate from Guadalcanal when their carriers were out of action, and Army Air Corps planes.

The Cactus air force pilots flew a gruelling schedule of sorties throughout the opening weeks of the campaign, intercepting bomber attacks and making

A Mitsubishi G4M1 of 705th Kokutai based at Rabaul, Philippines, in 1943.

79

A detailed view of the Mitsubishi G4M. During the latter stages of the war the plane was modified to carry the Ohka piloted bomb.

ground strikes on the Japanese forces which pressed in on the narrow beachhead. The airstrip was made of packed black dirt, which billowed in great clouds in the propeller backwash – clogging the eyes and nostrils of pilots, and also engines and gun ports. At night Japanese floatplanes (one was dubbed 'Washing Machine Charlie' because of the noise it made) would creep over to drop bombs – just to keep everyone awake and to further unsettle nerves already stretched taut. The diet, consisting mainly of canned spam and captured rice, was meagre, dysentery and malaria adding to the misery.

The Battle of the Eastern Solomons

The Japanese meanwhile had ordered a powerful counterstroke. Vice-Admiral Nobukate Kondo advanced southwards from Truk with the main striking power of the Combined Fleet, the carriers *Shokaku* and *Zuikaku*, the light carrier *Ryujo*, two battleships, several cruisers and destroyers, plus troop transports carrying reinforcements. To meet this threat Vice-Admiral Robert Ghormley, in overall command of US forces in the area, moved Vice-Admiral Fletcher's Task Force 61 up from Nouméa to waters east of the Solomons chain. Task Force 61 was formed around the carriers *Saratoga*, *Enterprise* and *Wasp*, with the new battleship, *North Carolina*.

On the morning of 23 August US reconnaissance aircraft spotted the Japanese fleet. SBDs and TBF torpedo-bombers from the *Saratoga* were put up, as well as land-based Marine aircraft from Henderson, but bad weather and a change of course by the transports thwarted an attempted strike. By the afternoon of that day Fletcher had lost the enemy

Above. Mitsubishi G4M 'Betty' bombers making a very low level attack on the US bridgehead during the Guadalcanal fighting, November 1942.

The Kawanishi H6K, a long-range Japanese maritime patrol aircraft, which was occasionally employed as a bomber.

Above. Japanese troop transports burn off the beaches of Guadalcanal, 16 November 1942. An SBD Dauntless flies by in the foreground.

fleet. Believing them to be much further north, he detached *Wasp* and her screening ships, sending them south to refuel. Kondo's 'Tokyo Express', however, was steaming at full speed towards Guadalcanal.

The clash came on the morning of the 24th, Kondo having pushed the light carrier *Ryujo* forward as bait. Aircraft from the *Ryujo* tried to knock out Henderson Field, but the defenders were already airborne and the Marine fighter pilots shot down 21 of the attackers. Meanwhile, 30 SBDs and six TBFs from *Enterprise* and *Saratoga* found the light carrier, plastering her with bombs and torpedoes. By mid-afternoon she was ablaze and sinking.

As the Americans concentrated on the *Ryujo*, the *Shokaku* and *Zuikaku* launched two successive strikes at the two US carriers, but Fletcher, mindful of the lessons of Midway and assisted by primitive but effective air-search radar on his ships, was ready with a heavy anti-aircraft screen in depth on the escort ships and with powerful combat air patrols (CAP) of Wildcats ready to pounce.

The CAP Wildcats met the Japanese Navy pilots 25 miles out from the targets. Several A5M Val dive-bombers and their protecting Zeros were shot down, but 24 got through, bearing down on the *Enterprise*. The sky was filled with billowing flak bursts and

streams of tracer, but the dive-bomber pilots flew on with the elan and precision of an elite force, peeling off at seven-second intervals to place three bombs squarely on the 'Big E'. One bomb sliced through the flight deck to explode in the crews' quarters, killing 30 men. Flames began to lick through the ship, but damage-control and fire-fighting teams held the fires in check. Within an hour the *Enterprise* was able to recover aircraft again. A steering failure followed, but this too was brought under control.

The fighting ended indecisively. The second Japanese strike, which included torpedo-carrying aircraft, took a wrong turn and missed its targets completely. The US aircraft, launched hastily by Fletcher's carriers as they prepared to receive the second Japanese strike, also failed to find the *Shokaku* and *Zuikaku*, but two of *Saratoga*'s SBD dive-bombers heavily damaged the seaplane-carrier *Chitose*.

Kondo's pilots returned, reporting damage to two enemy carriers and a battleship. The Japanese admiral decided to continue the engagement, taking two battleships and ten cruisers, together with escorting destroyers, south at high speed – but the US fleet had retired. SBDs from Henderson found this force, plastering the cruiser *Jinstu* and setting a transport ablaze. Eight B-17s flying from a base on Espiritu

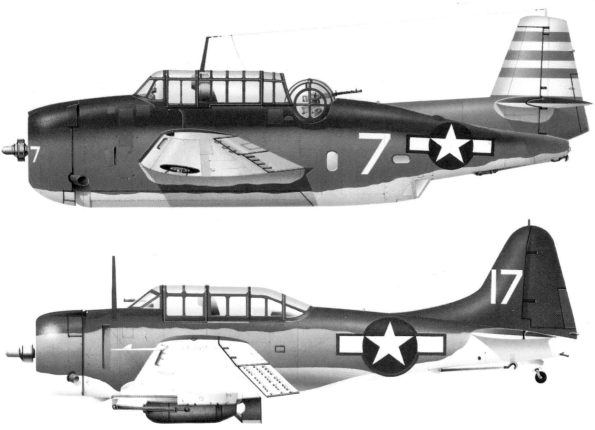

Top left. A US Navy Grumman TBF Avenger, which played a leading role in the Battle of Midway.

Below left. A Marine Corps Douglas SBD-4 Dauntless. The Dauntless was regarded as the most successful US dive-bomber of World War II.

Santo island joined the fight, managing to sink the destroyer *Mitsuki* in a high-level attack.

The battle for the Eastern Solomons had been won by a narrow margin by the Americans. The Japanese had lost a light carrier and many aircraft. The plan to isolate and pinch out the beachhead around Henderson Field had been thwarted. Nevertheless, the

Americans had made serious tactical errors, reconnaissance aircraft signally failed to find the Japanese fleet carriers and only luck had prevented the Japanese launching a second strike that could have been disastrous for the *Enterprise* and *Saratoga*.

The battle on the ground for Guadalcanal was still in the balance. Over the next two months both sides

Japanese aircraft warm up on the flight deck of the carrier *Akagi*.

Above. **The Vought OS2U Kingfisher observation floatplane, introduced in 1940 and widely used by the catapult flights of US Navy battleships and cruisers throughout the war.**

put reinforcements on the island, the Americans facing the growing risk of submarines in the eastern approaches to the Coral Sea. On 30 August the *Saratoga* was torpedoed and had to limp back to California for repairs. On 25 September the *Wasp*, assigned to cover a Marine troop convoy from Espiritu Santo island to Guadalcanal, was irreparably damaged by torpedoes from the submarine *I-19*. The *Hornet* was now the only operational carrier in the western Pacific.

The 'Tokyo Express' continued to operate each night as Japanese warships made their runs to bring men and supplies on to the island of Cape Esperance, shelling American positions as they transited Lunga Point. On one occasion two battleships sent shells plunging into Henderson Field, setting aviation fuel

tanks ablaze, cratering the strip and destroying 48 aircraft.

The Battle of Santa Cruz

The bold American campaign to seize Guadalcanal was floundering. The resupply of the beachhead was becoming prohibitively costly. Ashore, men were shivering with malaria, losing the will to fight. Admiral Nimitz admitted that the US Navy was unable to control the sea in the Cactus area. Nimitz named Admiral Halsey to replace Ghormley as commander of naval forces in the South Pacific and Rear-Admiral Thomas C. Kinkaid took over from Fletcher as commander of carrier operations.

A new Japanese offensive was launched on 25 October 1942. On land a massive push was made

Continued on page 89

The Mitsubishi Ki-46 'Dinah' was in service with the Japanese Army throughout the Pacific war as a high-altitude reconnaissance aircraft.

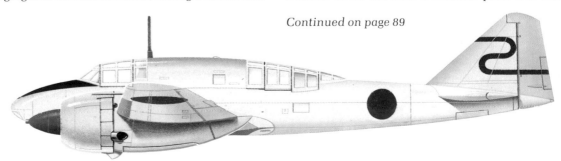

A shot-down Japanese Navy G4M 'Betty' bomber. The long-range G4M, with massive unprotected fuel tanks, was very vulnerable to attack.

Top left. A Bell P-400 Airacobra of the 67th Fighter Squadron, US Army Air Force, based in New Caledonia.

Left. A Lockheed P-38F Lightning, also based in New Caledonia. P-38s were responsible for the shooting down of the aircraft carrying Admiral Yamamoto.

Above. A B5N 'Jill' makes a torpedo run on the US battleship *South Dakota* at the Battle of Santa Cruz, 26 October 1942.

possible. At dawn a contact report was received from a scouting PBY. Admiral Halsey promptly gave the briefest of orders 'Attack-repeat-attack'.

Some 16 SBDs were flown off *Enterprise* on an armed scouting mission. Lt-Commander James R. Lee and his wingman, Ensign William E. Johnson, found the enemy fleet, just as eight A6M Zeros pounced. The dive-bomber crews actually managed to beat off the attack, shooting down three Zeros and escaping unscathed. Two SBDs, piloted by Lt Stickton B. Strong and Ensign Charles B. Irvine, penetrated the *Zuiho*'s fighter defences and planted a 500-lb bomb smack on her flight deck. Unable to recover her aircraft, the light carrier turned to limp home to Truk.

Both the US and Japanese carrier forces had launched strikes, which passed each other as they headed towards their respective targets. Zeros attacked the American formation, shooting down several Wildcats and Avengers at a cost of three of their own number, but it was the carriers which were their target. Coming in from 17,000 feet shortly after 0900, the Japanese dive-bombers broke though the US combat air patrol. The *Enterprise* was shrouded by a rain squall but the *Hornet* was exposed on the open ocean. As the dive-bombers wheeled in 25 were shot out of the air by anti-aircraft fire, but the *Hornet* was struck several times. A blazing A5M Val crashed right on to her flight deck. The *Enterprise* had now emerged from cover, but, protected by 40-mm anti-aircraft fire from her escorts, drove off the attackers, who managed to score only three minor hits. One bomb landed on the heavy armour of one of the battleship *South Dakota*'s forward turrets and another damaged the light cruiser *San Juan*.

About 180 miles to the northwest some of the *Hornet*'s aircraft had found the *Shokaku*. Dodging Zeros, the incoming SBDs went into their dives, planting four 1000-lb bombs on her sprawling, 850-foot-long flight deck. The accompanying TBF torpedo-bombers had lost formation and did not contribute to the attack. Nevertheless, the *Shokaku* was out of the battle – indeed she would be out of action and under extensive repair for nine months. The cruiser *Chikuma* was also roughly handled. The *Enterprise*'s strike force, its formations broken up in the encounter with Japanese fighters, was low on fuel by the time it reached the target area and its attacks were ineffectual.

Meanwhile damage control crews were bravely battling to save the *Hornet*. That afternoon A5M Kates from *Shokaku* hit her with two air-launched torpedoes, wrecking her engine-room. One of yet more attacking Kates made another torpedo hit and the order was given to abandon ship. Two accompanying US destroyers fired torpedoes at the stricken carrier, but she still refused to sink.

Kondo, sensing victory, sent surface forces forward to seek out and finish off the enemy, following with the undamaged *Zuikaku* and *Junyo*. As his cruisers neared the *Hornet*, with reconnaissance floatplanes flying ahead of them, the Americans strove frantically to finish off the *Hornet* with gunfire. Failing to do this, they withdrew. The shattered *Hornet* was at last despatched to the bottom by torpedoes fired by destroyers.

against the perimeter defence of Henderson Field while at sea a powerful striking force of five battleships and four carriers commanded by Admiral Nagumo took up stations to the northeast of the Santa Cruz islands. Nagumo's orders from the Combined Fleet Commander, Admiral Yamamoto, were simple: 'annihilate any powerful forces in the Solomons area.' Early on the 25th SBDs from the *Enterprise* began searching for the Japanese fleet. At midday a US flying boat sighted the enemy force northwest of the Santa Cruz islands, but the Japanese, realizing that they had been sighted, turned north – and the aircraft from the *Enterprise* undershot their track. A number of returning aircraft were damaged or, with empty fuel tanks, forced to ditch.

During the night of 25–26 October Nagumo's carriers steamed north. Meanwhile, the US task forces – Admiral Kinkaid's Task Force 61 built round the carrier *Enterprise*, and Admiral George Murray's Task Force 17, based on the *Hornet*, and Task Force 64 with the battleship *Washington* – were closing, intending to engage the enemy as soon as

A Nakajima B5N
'Kate' makes its
torpedo run during the
Battle of Santa Cruz.

The Battle of the Eastern Solomons had been a narrow victory for the Americans. The Japanese had redressed the balance off Santa Cruz by claiming the *Hornet* but Yamamoto had expended more than 100 aircraft and had lost many of his most experienced air crews, largely to anti-aircraft fire put up from escort ships. On Guadalcanal itself Henderson Field stayed in American hands.

The Japanese were still pouring troops into the island, while long-range G4M Bettys from Rabaul tried to hit US transports off the beachhead. On 13 November a task force commanded by Admiral Hiroake Abe, spearheaded by two battleships, the *Hiei* and the *Kirishima*, steamed down the 'Slot' to shell Henderson Field. The US cruiser force escorting the transports put up a determined fight. Two cruisers were sunk but the *Hiei* was crippled and Henderson reprieved once more. SBDs and TBFs of the Cactus air force and from the *Enterprise*, back in action in spite of a smashed flight deck elevator, sank the *Hiei*, the first Japanese battleship to be sent to the bottom during the war.

That night two Japanese cruisers shelled Henderson Field for half an hour. Revenge came the next day when US Marine and Navy aircraft sank six transports still trying to land ground reinforcements. On the evening of the following day (14 November) the battleships *South Dakota* and *Washington* battered the *Kirishima* so badly that she was scuttled by her crew, ending the last large-scale Japanese attempt to reinforce the garrison on Guadalcanal. Although the US Navy would suffer more losses, control of the sea around the island had at last been won – turning the besiegers into the besieged. Early in 1943 the Japanese began to evacuate the half-starved remnants of their forces. By 9 February the island was securely under American control.

Once again air power had proved decisive, not in an open-ocean carrier-to-carrier battle, but in gaining control of the sea in order to achieve a strategic objective on land. Land- and carrier-based US air power had worked in concert to achieve victory in the first American offensive of the Pacific war. The Japanese had lost 893 land- and ship-based aircraft. Equally important, 2362 naval airmen – the veteran, elite aircrews of the Combined Fleet who had tasted victory for so long – were now lying at the bottom of the ocean.

Above. A US Army Air Force B-17D on a mission over the Solomons in October 1942.

Right. The Douglas SBD Dauntless was highly successful. A total of 5936 was built from 1940 to the SBD-6 model of 1943. It was the principal air weapon during the battles of Coral Sea and Midway, and in the Solomon Islands campaign.

A Japanese aircraft is shot down while attempting to attack the USS *Kitkun Bay*.

CHAPTER 6

AMERICA ON THE OFFENSIVE

The Build-up of US Naval Air Power

Throughout the months of bitter struggle for Guadalcanal, there had been times when the US naval air power in the western Pacific had hinged on the availability of just one carrier. Now in the first six months of 1943 no fewer than nine new fast carriers were preparing to join the US Pacific fleet, four of them of the 27,000-ton *Essex* class, which could accommodate over 80 new-generation aircraft.

Bigger and heavier than their 1930s antecedents, the *Essex* class incorporated such improvements as better hull compartmentalization, heavier, close-in anti-aircraft armament and air-search radar. An important change was the inclusion of three elevators in the design which enabled aircraft to be manoeuvred in and out of the hangar deck more quickly.

The other new carriers were of the smaller *Independence* class, originally laid down as light cruisers. Nine *Independence*-class ships were commissioned between January and December 1943, each with a standard displacement of 11,000 tons and capacity for 45 aircraft. At 610 feet overall, they were 245 feet shorter than the *Essex* class, although marginally faster. To distinguish them from their big sisters, the members of the class were redesignated Small Aircraft Carriers (CVL) in 1943 and were officially referred to as light carriers.

Very large numbers of new types of aircraft were also joining the Navy, Marine Corps and Army Air Force squadrons in the Pacific. P-38s and early-model P-51s and P-47Ds were reaching Army Air Force fighter squadrons in the Pacific theatre, but it was a new generation of carrier aircraft that were to be at the cutting edge of the first great offensives launched in 1943 against the Japanese perimeter. By the middle of that year the US Navy had about 18,000 aircraft. By the end of 1944 it could muster no less than 30,000 of all types.

The hard combat lessons of 1941–2 had been thoroughly assimilated and had led to the creation of some very combat-capable hardware. From January 1943 onwards the Grumman F6F Hellcat superseded

Top left. A Lockheed P-38J Lightning of 432nd Fighter Squadron, US Army Air Force, based in New Guinea in late 1943.
Below left. A Douglas A-24B Dauntless of the 312th Bomb Group, US Army Air Force, based in the Gilbert Islands in December 1943.

the Wildcat in US Navy fighter squadrons except aboard escort carriers. The TBF Avenger had replaced the elderly Devastator in the torpedo-carrying role and the big Curtiss SB2C Helldiver was supplanting the SBD Dauntless scout/dive-bomber.

The Helldiver, the first US dive-bomber with an internal bomb-bay, could theoretically carry a torpedo, but the conversion of the bomb racks took several hours. The Grumman TBF Avenger had made its combat debut at Midway, but after a disastrous opening in which five of six TBFs had been shot down, the aircraft continued successfully in the torpedo-strike and light-bomber role and made very valuable contributions to the air battles of 1943. The Helldiver, in contrast, suffered from numerous design troubles, some stemming from the original requirement that two Hellcats with wings folded should fit the standard US Navy carrier elevator. The Helldiver's barrel-chested fuselage was thus kept as short as possible, prejudicing lateral stability. The aircraft, dubbed the 'Beast' by its crews, was also overweight. Although it was put into mass production in 1941, it did not enter combat until the end of 1943 and was not considered fully combat-worthy until improved versions appeared a year later.

Marine Corps pilots were also beginning to make good use of the big Vought F4U Corsair's ground-attack potential. The gull-winged, radial-engined F4U was already a controversial aircraft, designed to meet a 1938 US Navy requirement for a high-speed, single-seat shipboard fighter. The resulting machine was judged to be too big, heavy and 'bouncy' for carrier operations but production aircraft went to Marine Corps squadrons, who quickly learned to put them to good use. The pilots had completed only some 20 hours conversion training when they were sent to join the beleaguered US air squadrons on Guadalcanal. There were 12 F4U-1s in the first batch of aircraft of Marine Fighter Squadron VMF-124 to arrive on the island on 12 February 1943.

The first combat mission was not auspicious. On 14 February F4U-1 Corsairs of VMF-124 flew escort to a formation of US Navy PB4Y Liberator long-range bombers making a raid on Bougainville. Some 50 Zeros rose to intercept and made mincemeat of the attackers, shooting down four Army Air Force P-38 Lightnings flying top cover, two P-40s, two of the bombers and two Corsairs – all for the loss of four Japanese fighters. But the Marine pilots, becoming ever more familiar with the potential of the Chance-Vought fighter, soon established air superiority in the Solomons. By the end of 1943 all Marine Corps fighter squadrons in the South Pacific were equipped with Corsairs.

A Curtiss SB2C Helldiver belonging to VB-17, on board the USS *Bunker Hill*, November 1943.

Above. **The Vought F4U-1 Corsair was first rejected as too big and too heavy for carrier operations by the US Navy but was soon put to outstanding use by US Marine pilots flying ground-attack missions. Carrier service began in late 1944.**

doomed aircraft plunged into the jungle below.

Yamamoto's death symbolized the humbling of Japanese power. By the spring of 1943 not only had its onward momentum been checked, but US forces were now poised to make dramatic advances themselves in the 'island-hopping' campaign which combined land, sea and air operations – in a way and on a scale never before practised in warfare. The exercise of air power was critical. Each island captured represented an airstrip to be cleared or scraped out of the jungle from which the assault on the next island in the chain could be supported, and so on. In this kind of warfare, the bulldozers of the Seabees were as important an offensive weapon as the aircraft which eventually flew from the newly created airstrips themselves.

Henderson Field on Guadalcanal was the first such vital toehold. From February 1943 onwards aircraft from Henderson Field were able to cover the US ground forces as they doggedly fought their way up the island chain to Bougainville itself, which was captured on 1 November 1943.

Across the Solomon Sea was the Japanese naval base at Rabaul, the operational centre for all air force units in what the Japanese called the Southeastern Area. Rabaul, at the eastern end of New Britain, was too tough a target for an amphibious assault, but it was the object of a prolonged air offensive, just before which, in September 1943, it was home to about 300 aircraft of the 11th Air Fleet. In addition, at Truk, almost 800 miles away in the Caroline Islands, there were two carrier air groups ready to reinforce Rabaul if necessary.

The first major strike against Rabaul was made on 12 October 1943 by 349 aircraft of the US 5th Air Force, the Army Air Force keeping up the offensive in further day and night raids. Then, on 5 November, Admiral Halsey launched an all-out carrier-based attack on Rabaul. Task Force 38, centred on the USS *Saratoga* and the new *Independence*-class carrier *Princeton*, launched 97 strike aircraft. Defensive combat air patrol over the US carriers was provided by land-based aircraft from Henderson, while first the Hellcat fighters, then the TBFs and SB2Cs, came in to hit the shipping which packed the shallow harbour.

The Hellcats encountered a flock of over 70 defending Zeros but the new naval fighters quickly asserted their superiority. Ensign Robert W. Duncan of VF-5, flying from the *Yorktown*, had become the first Hellcat pilot to down a Zero during a mission against the great naval base at Truk the month before.

Admiral Yamamoto had warned of America's industrial potential before the attack on Pearl Harbor. Now, on the morning of 18 April 1943, the admiral was flying in one of a pair of G4M Betty bombers to Bougainville for a tour of inspection. Alerted to his movements through their breaking of the Japanese naval code, the Americans sprang an elaborate trap, when 16 Army Air Force P-38 long-range fighters fell out of the sun, their nose gun batteries blazing. Yamamoto's aircraft was riddled with bullets, flames erupted from an engine, one of the bomber's long, slender wings broke off, and the

Continued on page 98

A Vought F4U-2 Corsair of the US Marine Corps, based on Roi Island in the Kwajalein group in 1944.

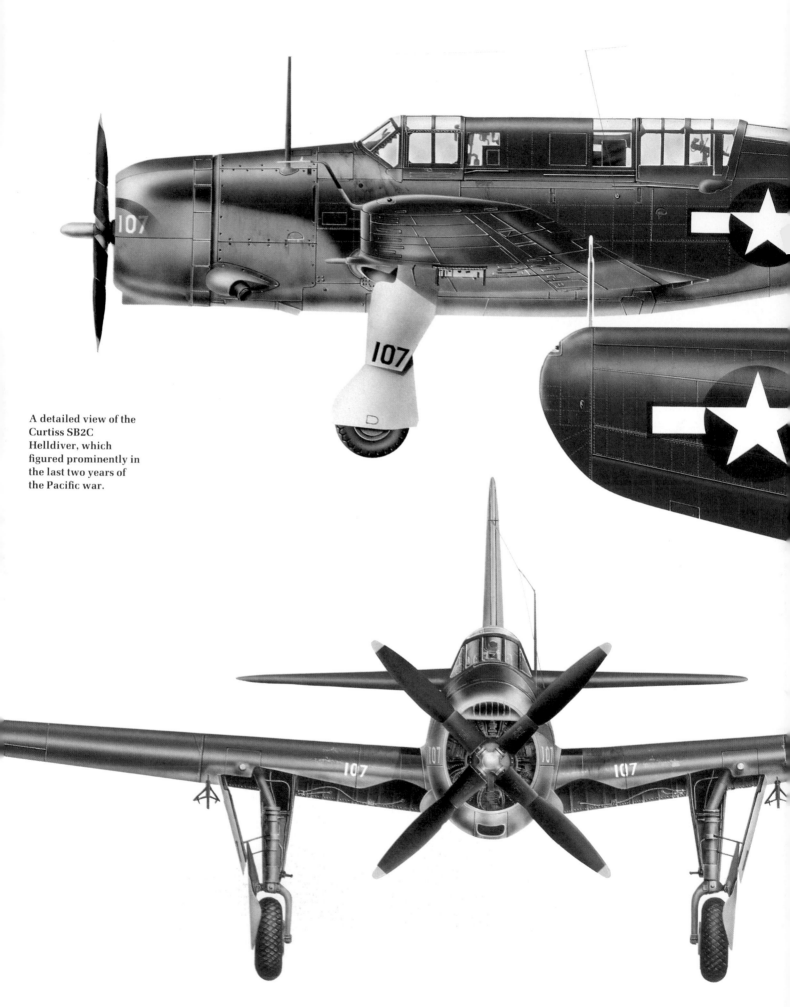

A detailed view of the Curtiss SB2C Helldiver, which figured prominently in the last two years of the Pacific war.

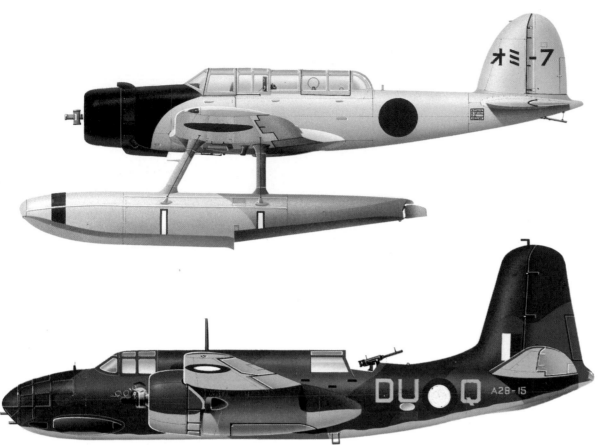

Top left. The Aichi E13A, a long-range reconnaissance floatplane, entered service with the Japanese Navy in late 1941.

Below left. A Douglas Boston Mk III of No. 22 Squadron, Royal Australian Air Force, based in New Guinea in March 1943.

On this occasion 25 Japanese aircraft were shot down and an equal number of probables claimed. The attackers lost just ten aircraft.

The 'easy' victory at Rabaul set the pattern for future carrier-based strikes. Alarmed by these activities, the Japanese flew in 100 aircraft from Truk, thus further depleting their carrier air group reserves.

As the campaign in the Solomons slowly progressed, a fresh axis of advance in the central Pacific was opened up, with the newly organized Central Pacific Force (later the 5th Fleet) as the battering ram. Under the command of Admiral Chester Nimitz's former chief-of-staff, Vice-Admiral Raymond Spruance, the new fleet could muster six large and six light carriers, a sizeable screen of cruisers and destroyers, and oilers, tenders and supply ships. In the van of this powerful group was Task Force 58, commanded by Rear-Admiral Marc A. Mitscher, the pugnacious former captain of the *Hornet*, and himself a pioneer from the earliest days of US naval aviation.

The thrust westwards across the central Pacific towards Japan began with Operation Galvanic. Launched on 23 November 1943, this ended successfully with the capture of Tarawa and Makin islands in the Gilberts after weeks of bitter fighting, spearheaded by carrier-based, close-support air strikes. During operations on the Gilberts TBF crews from VT-6 used air-to-surface radar to enable the Hellcats to intercept Japanese night intruders. The first attempt at a night interception, on 25 November, was unsuccessful. The next night two Hellcats failed to locate enemy aircraft but the pilot of the lead Avenger, Lt-Commander John Philips, shot down two G4M Betty bombers in the dark with his single, forward-firing machine-gun. Sad to relate, as the planes were feeling their way back in the dark, the Avenger's rear gunner shot down the Hellcat of the *Enterprise*'s air group commander, Lt-Commander Edward ('Butch') O'Hare, the fighter ace and veteran of the earliest Pacific air war battles.

Leapfrogging forward from the Gilberts, Spruance next implemented Operation Flintlock, the capture

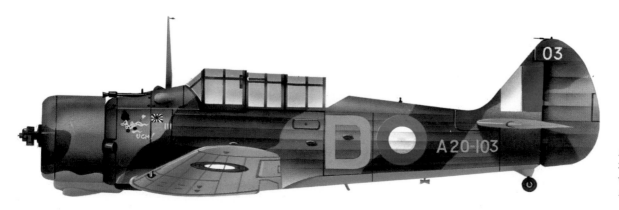

A Commonwealth CA-3 Wirraway in service with the Royal Australian Air Force.

Above. **F6F Hellcat lands aboard the new Essex-class carrier USS *Lexington* during operations off Saipan.**

of Kwajalein and Eniwetok in the Marshalls. On 17 February 1944 Task Force 58's carriers struck at Truk itself, the base of the Japanese Combined Fleet on Dublom island in the central Carolines. The fleet was now commanded by Admiral Mineichi Koga, the successor to Yamamoto. Koga had evacuated most of his major warships to Palau, but there were still transports in the harbour. The Hellcats fell on the island's airstrips, destroying aircraft on the ground and shooting down 30 of those which managed to get into the air. Avengers strewed fragmentation bombs on aircraft dispersals, barracks and headquarters buildings, while dive-bombers consigned the transports in the harbour to fiery ruin. During the night 12 radar-equipped TBF-C Avengers from VT-10 aboard *Enterprise* flew the first night attack from a carrier of the war. One aircraft was shot down but the others sank or damaged 13 Japanese ships. Truk would now be allowed to 'wither on the vine' – kept under constant air harassment in order to deny its use to the enemy as a fleet base.

The Battle of the Philippines Sea

Bypassing Truk, Nimitz now made a 1000-mile leap across the western Pacific to Guam, Saipan and

Tinian in the Marianas. Establishing airbases here would bring the Japanese home islands themselves within range of long-range B-29 bombers.

A second important objective of the Marianas campaign was to lure the Combined Fleet out of its improvised base in northeastern Borneo and into action. Since the air-sea battles off Santa Cruz, the Japanese, too, had been rebuilding their carrier strength and re-equipping the air wings. New carriers such as the 30,000-ton *Taiho* featured armoured flight decks. The new model A6M5b Zero at last carried some armour protection for pilots and self-sealing fuel tanks. The Yokosuka D4Y2 Judy had supplanted the obsolete Val dive-bombers and the Nakajima B6N carrier torpedo-bomber had likewise replaced the long-serving B5N Kate. But although Japanese industry was still capable of turning out large numbers of technically sophisticated aircraft (16,600 in 1943, 28,100 in 1944), the real problem was availability of aircrew. The air battles in the Solomons had frittered away the lives of the veteran pilots of 1941–42. Although there was no shortage of fanatically brave young men to replace them, providing the new pilots with enough training to give them a chance in combat was another matter.

On receiving news of the landings at Saipan, Admiral Jisaburo Ozawa led the powerful 1st Mobile Fleet northeastwards. His force consisted of the carriers *Shokaku*, *Zuikaku* and *Taiho*, the medium carriers *Hiyo* and *Junyo*, and the light carriers *Zuiho*, *Ryujo*, *Chitose* and *Chiyoda*, escorted by a powerful surface warfare group of battleships and cruisers. In all the Japanese had around 475 aircraft. Ozawa's objective was to relieve Saipan, crush the bridgehead and destroy the invasion fleet.

To meet him Spruance could deploy 891 aircraft flying from 15 carriers and light carriers, divided into four task groups. Six fast modern battleships, normally part of the carrier task groups, had been detached and formed into a fifth task group, the so-called Battle Line. Although Spruance was aboard a ship of Task Force 58 he left its supremo, Admiral Mitscher, in tactical command.

On 17 June Spruance gave Mitscher his battle plan. 'Our air will first knock out enemy carriers, then will attack enemy battleships and cruisers to slow or disable them. Battle Line will destroy enemy fleet either by fleet action if the enemy elects to fight or by sinking slowed or crippled ships if enemy retreats. Action against the enemy must be pushed vigorously by all hands to ensure complete destruction of the fleet.'

Ozawa approached from the southwest with his fleet divided into two parts – a van force including three light carriers, and the main body formed around six carriers, 100 miles to the rear. On the afternoon of 18 June Japanese reconnaissance aircraft spotted Task Force 58, 200 miles west of Saipan. The van force, commanded by Admiral Kurita, moved to a position outside the combat radius of the American carrier aircraft. He was relying on a slight advantage in range of his own aircraft in order to mount an ambitious attack that involved aircraft hitting the US fleet, then continuing on to Guam where they would refuel and rearm for a second strike. Land-based aircraft from Guam were also to join in the attack.

Early on the morning of 19 June the flight decks of the Japanese carriers throbbed with the sound and vibration of massed aero-engines warming up. More than 300 brand-new, modern strike aircraft and fighters, flown by highly dedicated young pilots, were waved off the carriers in five groups into a fine, clear sky. Meanwhile, dive-bombers were reported to be taking off from Orote Field on Guam. Accordingly, 33 Hellcats were despatched from the *Lexington* to the island to deal with them, shooting down or destroying on the ground about 30 Japanese aircraft. At 1000 hours came the recall order – air warning radar had picked up a bunch of incoming

Continued on page 104

Above. Aircraft with wings folded aboard the USS *Ticonderoga* in June 1944. *Left.* A Curtiss SB2C-1 Helldiver of VB-8 aboard the USS *Bunker Hill.*

A detailed view of the Vought F4U Corsair, considered the finest shipborne fighter of the Pacific war.

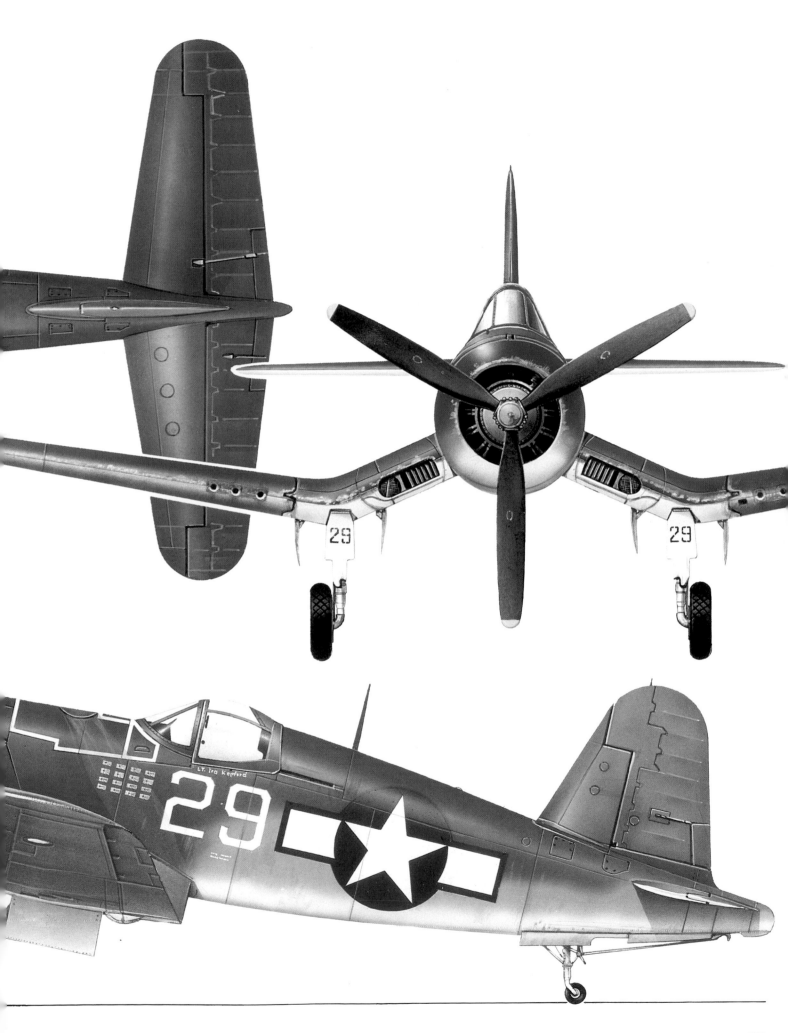

aircraft at a range of 140 miles. Ozawa had launched his first strike of 69 aircraft at 0830 and about 30 minutes later the second wave of 128 aircraft got into the air.

Every Hellcat that could fly was ordered into the air. To clear the flight decks to enable the combat air patrols to land, refuel and rearm, Mitscher ordered his strike aircraft into the air. Out of range and unable to make a useful sortie against the Japanese fleet, they were to stand off on the eastern, unengaged flank of the task force.

With ample radar warning and guided to their intercept positions by radio, the Hellcats climbed to 25,000 feet, forming up in waves ready to pounce.

In air-to-air combat the Hellcat could stay with the lighter Zero through most manoeuvres, but the Grumman could not follow its opponent in a tight loop. When following a Zero in a close turn, a Hellcat pilot would often be forced to roll out in order to avoid a stall.

A manoeuvre adopted by Japanese pilots to throw off a Hellcat on their tail was to execute a snap split-S to port at low altitude, pulling through over the open ocean. With a Zero on his tail, a US Navy pilot would take advantage of the Hellcat's superior speed to dive and twist away using the ailerons. In level flight the Hellcat could generally exploit its speed advantage to pull away, and its rugged airframe could absorb bursts of 7.7-mm machine-gun fire. One burst from the six 0.5-inch guns of the Hellcat was usually enough to set a Zero ablaze.

As their pilots pushed the charging handles of their machine-guns forward, 140 Hellcats nosed down on the incoming Japanese aircraft spread out over the sprawling blue ocean below them. The US Navy planes ripped through the Japanese formations. The raw Japanese pilots were brave enough but their flying skills were a mere shadow of those of the generation who had been expended in the Solomons battles.

Japanese aircraft 'fell like leaves', said one pilot. Those that survived the attacks by the Hellcats hit a curtain of anti-aircraft fire thrown up by the Battle Line, which included shells tipped with the new proximity fuse. These had only to get near in order to bring down their target. The sole bomb hit was on the *South Dakota*. A total of 42 Japanese aircraft were brought down. None reached the carriers and only one US aircraft was shot down.

Some 30 minutes later the second Japanese strike wave was brought to battle, David McCampbell, commanding the *Essex's* air group, led his squadron VF-15 into a stacked formation of Yokosuka D4Y Judy dive bombers, shooting down four and claiming

one probable before exhausting his ammunition. Later the same day McCampbell claimed three more enemy aircraft. By the end of the war he was the Navy's leading ace with 34 victories, for which he was awarded the Congressional Medal of Honor.

Only 20 aircraft broke through the US fighter screen – to be brought down by anti-aircraft fire. Six D4Y Judys fought their way through to reach the *Wasp* and the *Bunker Hill*, but did little damage. Suddenly the sky was empty of Japanese aircraft.

This was what Lt-Commander Paul Buie, the leader of VF-16, dubbed the 'Great Marianas Turkey Shoot', a crushing defeat for the Japanese Navy's air arm. Of the 109 planes which attacked the task force

Above. **Admiral Marc Mitscher, veteran Navy pilot and commander of Fast Carrier Task Force 58 from January 1944.**

A Curtiss Kittyhawk Mk IV of No. 80 Squadron, Royal Australian Air Force, based in the Moluccas in 1942.

Above. The Consolidated PB2Y Coronado was used extensively as a patrol flying boat by the US Navy.

that morning, only about 15 survived. But Admiral Ozawa still believed that his air groups had flown on to land on Marianas airstrips as planned and he continued to feed aircraft into the battle. A third strike of 49 aircraft was launched but the main body of this force failed to find the US fleet and returned to their carriers. The others were jumped by Hellcats, seven being shot down. A fourth, 82-strong wave, followed, but it, too, suffered a catastrophe. Those aircraft which survived the devastating attacks by the fighters that screened the US carriers fled to Guam, only to be shot up a they tried to land. At 1300 the bomb-armed Helldivers and Avengers that had been loitering east of the carriers were ordered to bomb the Guam airstrip. Only nine Japanese aircraft survived.

No US air strike could yet be aimed at the Japanese carriers but shortly before midday the submarine USS *Cavalla* had slipped through the enemy escorts and fired three torpedoes at the *Shokaku*. The carrier caught fire and three hours later she blew up. The *Taiho*, too, was irretrievably damaged by torpedoes. Fumes from a shattered fuel line were ignited and the ship's armoured flight deck peeled open like a tin can in the intense heat.

Ozawa had lost two carriers and almost 400

Japanese aircraft had been swatted out the sky. Mitscher had lost 23 aircraft; his fleet was virtually unscathed. But the Japanese admiral still had seven carriers afloat and a reserve of 100 aircraft. Believing that the US fleet had been badly mauled and that his air groups had escaped to Guam, that night he ordered a retirement to the northwest to refuel, planning to renew the battle at first light the next day, the 21st. Late on the 20th a signal intercepted from an American reconnaissance aircraft told Ozawa that he had been located and that he could now expect an attack. He ordered an increase in speed to get out of range of any attack that might be launched in the fading daylight – but too late.

Admiral Spruance, weighing the chances that the Japanese could not now break through and attack the Saipan bridgehead, had ordered Mitscher to close the range and take the offensive.

Mitscher faced a terrible dilemma. The sun was setting fast on the western horizon. If a strike was launched now, his aircraft would have to locate and attack the enemy ships in twilight and return to attempt deck landings in the dark – if they could find their own ships. Such an operation would stretch navigation and flying skills to the limit, but if a launch was delayed until daylight the enemy might

A Commonwealth CA-2 Boomerang of the Royal Australian Air Force in New Guinea in 1944.

Opposite. A defending Japanese Navy B6N 'Jill' torpedo bomber hurls itself at the USS *Yorktown* during operations off Truk, April 1944.

slip out of reach. 'Launch 'em' declared the grizzled admiral.

The US carrier's decks exploded into action. Hellcats and bomb-laden Avengers and Helldivers – 216 aircraft in all – were hurled into the air, heading west into the sunset in an attempt to catch Ozawa before he drew out of range into the darkness. With the light fading fast they found the Japanese fleet. Ozawa managed to get 75 aircraft up but they were as ineffective in defence as they had been in attack. The carrier *Hiyo* was mortally hit. The *Zuikaku* was severely damaged and set on fire, as was the *Chiyoda*. The battleship *Haruna* and a heavy cruiser were damaged and two of the tankers that were to have refuelled the fleet were sunk. In all 65 Japanese aircraft were shot down at a cost of 20 American planes. The Japanese fleet withdrew towards Okinawa to lick its wounds. Barely 30 aircraft were left out of a fleet of 400 that had set off so vaingloriously the previous morning to smash the Americans.

The airborne strike force began to form up, turning round in the darkness to grope its way back towards the carriers. As softly illuminated instrument panels glowed gently in darkened cockpits, fuel gauges began to dip and the ocean below turned into inky blackness. On the carriers the crew could hear returning aircraft droning overhead, some flashing recognition lights, others with their engines spluttering as fuel tanks ran dry. There were ominous thumps as aircraft ditched in the sea.

Some seasoned pilots made successful landings on the blacked-out carriers. Others could make out the white wakes of the big ships, but could not distinguish the flat-tops from the cruisers. One aircraft even tried to land on a destroyer.

Again Admiral Mitscher had to make a fateful decision – to illuminate the fleet's landing lights and risk a submarine attack, or watch his aircraft end up

in the sea. He made up his mind to turn on the lights.

The carriers switched on their red mast-head running lights – the flight decks were outlined, searchlights lit up the sky, beckoning to the incoming pilots, and starshell was fired from 5-inch guns. By 2200 every aircraft had been either landed or had ditched in the sea. Over 80 were lost this way and in deck crash-landings. Ships and floatplanes combed the area all night for ditched aircrew, safely picking up the vast majority of them. Task Force 58 turned back for the Marianas. The last 'classic' carrier-to-carrier battle of the Pacific war was over.

US Army Air Force Operations

While the carrier-borne air power of the US Navy was tearing huge holes in the Japanese defence perimeter in the great battles of 1942–3, the US Army Air Force was building up immense strength on land. When the battered survivors of the Philippines-based Far East Air Forces reached Australia early in 1942, they were reorganized to form the nucleus of a new US 5th Air Force, whose aircraft began to fly offensive reconnaissance and strike missions during the Battle of the Coral Sea and the Solomons fighting. Commanded from August 1942 by Lt-General G.C. Kenney, the 5th Air Force was committed to the bitter fighting for New Guinea where Australian and US forces fought first to halt the Japanese advance on Port Moresby and then to evict the Japanese themselves.

As well as bombing enemy ground forces and airstrips, aircraft flew troops and supplies from Australia to Port Moresby and then across the Owen Stanley mountains. Anti-shipping strikes on Japanese reinforcement convoys became a speciality. During the Battle of the Bismarck Sea on 2–4 March 1943, P-38s, A-20s, B-17s and B-25s of the 5th Air Force, operating with Royal Australian Air Force

A Supermarine Spitfire Mk VIII of 457 Squadron, the Royal Australian Air Force, 1943.

Beaufighters, made low-altitude attacks that sank every ship in a 22-strong convoy.

The 5th Air Force turned its attention to Ewak and Rabaul and was heavily engaged in the conquest of Hollandia in April 1944. At the same time the 5th's aircraft had spearheaded advances to the western-most point of New Guinea, where General Douglas MacArthur stood poised for an invasion of Moroia and his promised return to the Philippines. While in training, the 5th was put under the command of Major-General Ennis C. Whitehead, and incorporated with 13th Air Force in General Kenney's new Far East Air Forces.

The 13th Air Force had been formed in December 1942 to support operations on the Solomons. In the Guadalcanal campaign, ground attack with cannon-armed P-39 Airacobras became a speciality and it was P-38 Lightnings of the 13th which shot down Yamamoto. B-24 long-range bomber units attacked Rabaul and Kavieng and, as new airstrips were

seized, fresh targets were brought within range. B-24s took off from the northernmost Solomons to fly 13-hour over-water missions to attack Truk. With the powerful naval base of Truk effectively neutralized, the 13th's heavy bombers were switched westwards to assist the 5th Air Force in softening up Noemfoor Island for a successful assault in July 1944. In June 1944 B-24 strikes on Yap cut the link between Japanese positions in the south and the Marianas to facilitate the capture of Saipan. The Army Air Force then turned its attention to attacks on the Palaus for

the September 1944 invasion of the Philippines.

The 7th Air Force was formed in February 1942 from the smashed remnants of the Hawaiian Air Force. B-17s and B-26s made brave but futile attacks during the Battle of Midway and a B-17 Group took part in the Solomons Campaign. B-24s and B-17s of the 7th attacked Wake and other Japanese island outposts in support of the central Pacific drive across the Gilberts and Marshalls to the Marianas. Flying from bases in the Ellice Islands, the 7th made many sorties against Tarawa, Makin, Nauru, Wotje, Aluit,

Above left. General Douglas MacArthur, who commanded Allied forces in the Southwest Pacific area in World War II.

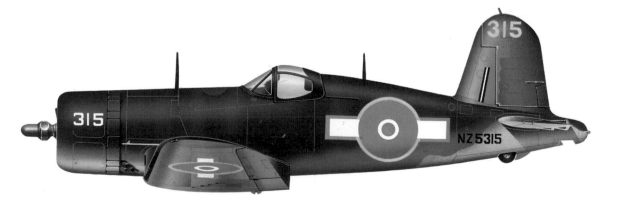

A Vought F4U-1A Corsair of 17 Squadron, Royal New Zealand Air Force, based at Guadalcanal in August 1944.

Continued on page 113

Above. SBD dive-bombers head for Rabaul, the important Japanese base at the eastern end of New Britain, captured in January 1942. From October 1943 it was subjected to constant raids by land- and carrier-based US aircraft.

Maloelap and Kwajalein. The fall of Tarawa in November 1943 provided bases for further long-range strikes against the Marshalls.

As the tide of the offensive swept westwards, 7th Air Force aircraft flew 'milk-runs' against bypassed Japanese bases in the Marshalls, and also delivered blows on Truk, Ponape, Kusaie, and Eniwetok. Ground-attacking P-47 fighter-bombers joined in the June 1944 assault on Saipan. The capture of Guam and Tinian in July provided bases for further strikes on the Volcano and Bonin Islands.

In the northern Pacific, meanwhile, the 11th Air Force was fighting an almost forgotten campaign in

defence of Alaska and the Aleutian Islands. There were three quick changes of title as the Alaskan Defence Command of 1941 became the Alaskan Air Force in January 1942 and then the 11th Air Force in February. As part of the Midway campaign the Japanese made diversionary raids on Dutch Harbor and landed detachments on the remote islands of Attu and Kiska in the Aleutian chain. The 11th, commanded by Major General William O. Butler, responded by bombing the Japanese-held islands from bases on the previously uninhabited island of Amchitka, occupied in January 1943.

Operating in the fog and sub-zero temperatures of

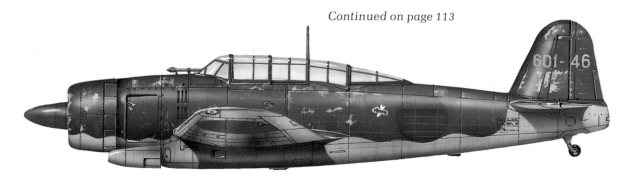

The Yokosuka D4Y3 Suisei was a single-engined carrier-based dive-bomber which never achieved its full potential.

A detailed view of the
Lockheed PV-1
Ventura, an American
medium bomber
which served with
other Allied air forces.

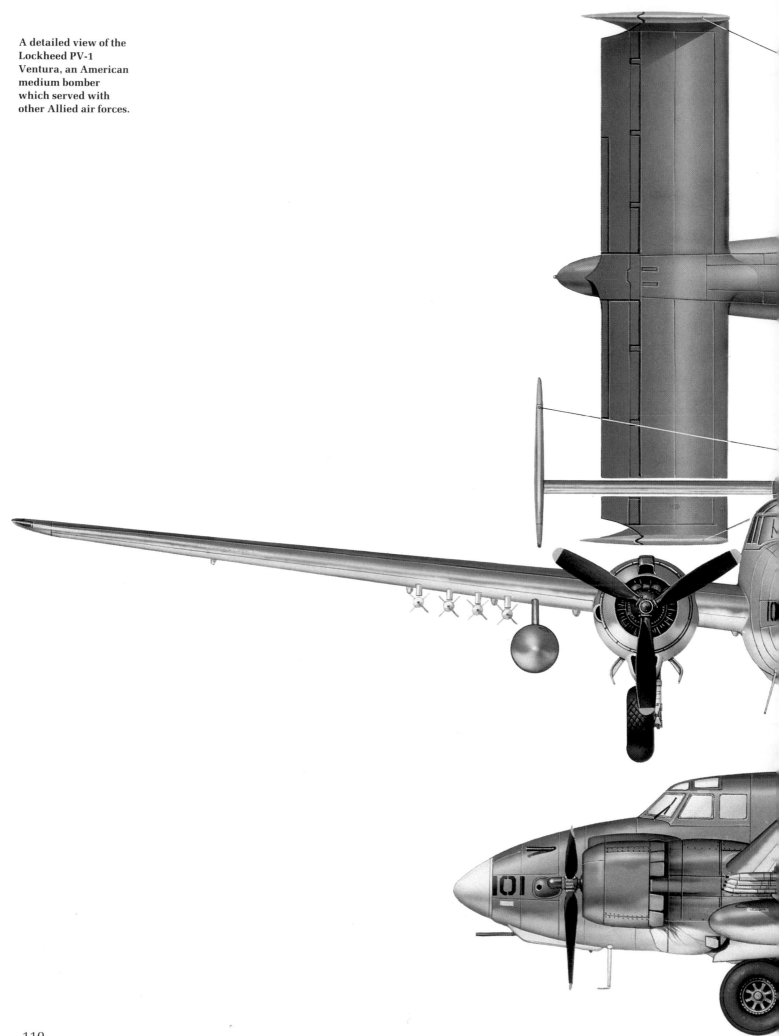

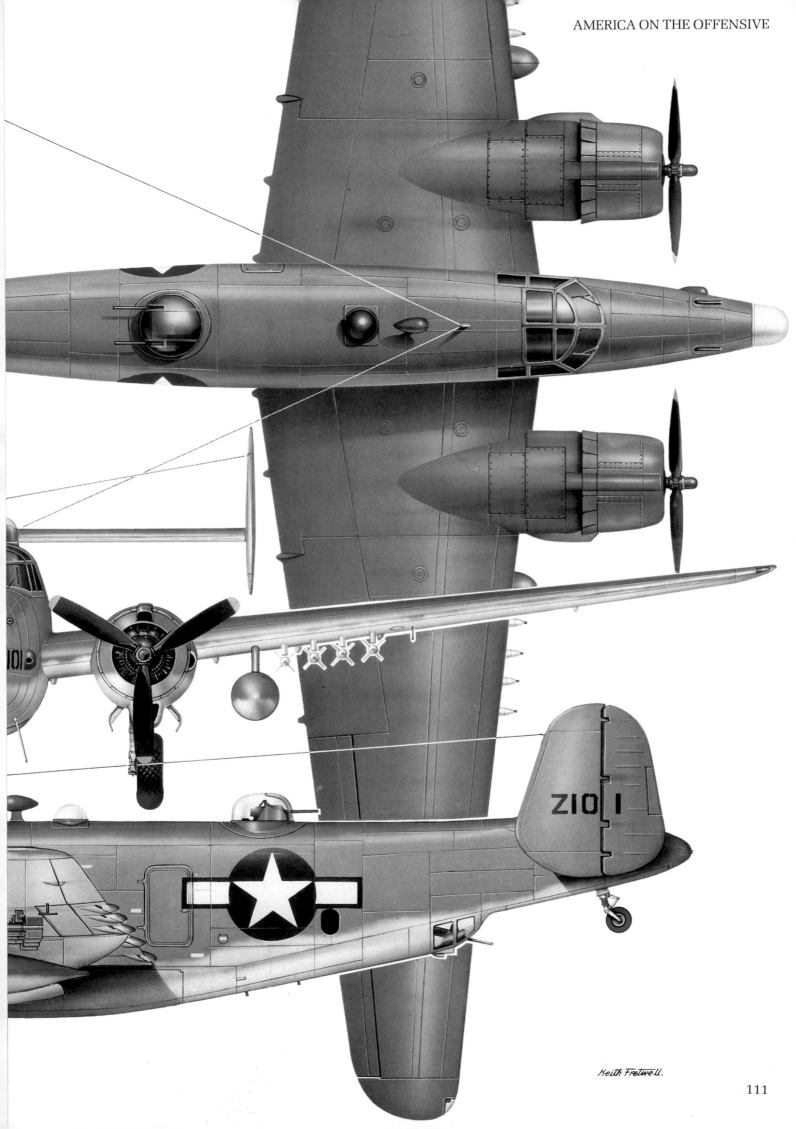

Keith Fretwell.

US Army Air Force Curtiss P-40s in action over the bleak tundra of Kiska island in the Aleutians. The island was occupied by the Japanese on 7 June 1942, then evacuated a year later.

on Leyte itself, air cover would be provided by Admiral Halsey's 3rd Fleet, with over a 1000 carrier-borne aircraft, and by the escort carriers of Vice-Admiral Thomas C. Kinkaid's 7th Fleet, which had the immediate mission of transporting and supplying the invasion force.

Opposing these very powerful naval forces was Admiral Soemu Toyoda's Combined Fleet. The major combat units, each independent and responsible to Toyoda, were Vice-Admiral Kurita's 1st Striking Force of battleships, cruisers, and destroyers based near Singapore, Vice-Admiral Kiohide Shima's 2nd Striking Force based in the north of Japan and the carriers of Vice-Admiral Jisaburo Ozawa's Main Body, riding at anchor in the Inland Sea. Under separate command but also reporting to Toyoda were the Japanese Navy's air units in the Philippines. Lt-General Kyoji Tominaga, commanding the 4th Air Army on the Philippines, had no command link with his naval counterpart, apart from at Imperial General Headquarters level.

This fissure in the command system proved dangerous to the Sho plan right from the very beginning. In mid-October Halsey's air groups began softening-up strikes on Japanese bases in an arc from the Philippines to the Ryukyus. On 12 October they hit Formosa. Admiral Shigero Fukudome, commanding the Japanese Navy's air defences, reported later: 'Our fighters were nothing but so many eggs thrown at the stone wall of the indomitable enemy formations. In a brief one-sided encounter the combat terminated in our total defeat.'

Toyoda independently directed the Navy's air units to implement Sho, believing that the invasion had already begun. The Japanese Army Air Force, meanwhile, stayed on the ground as Navy pilots were swatted out of the sky by Halsey's Hellcats. Over 600 Japanese aircraft were lost.

When the invasion actually did begin, on 17 October, the Japanese High Command was wrong-footed. On the evening of the 18th Imperial General Headquarters directed the Sho operation to be put

Opposite above. The Battle of Leyte Gulf.
Opposite below. A Curtiss SO3C-1 Seagull scout fitted with a spatted undercarriage.

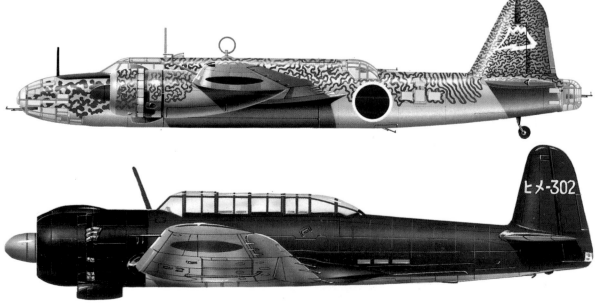

Top left. A Nakajima Ki-49-II Donryu. The aircraft was used by the Japanese Army Air Force in China and New Guinea, but its performance was generally poor.
Left. A Nakajima B6N2 Tenzan, a carrier-based torpedo bomber. The type was intensively used during the last two years of the war.

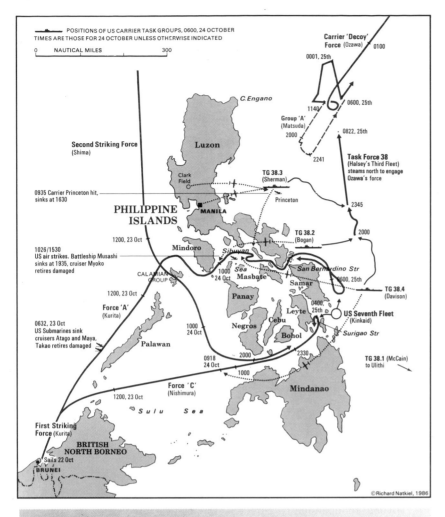

POSITIONS OF US CARRIER TASK GROUPS, 0600, 24 OCTOBER
TIMES ARE THOSE FOR 24 OCTOBER UNLESS OTHERWISE INDICATED

0   NAUTICAL MILES   300

Carrier 'Decoy' Force (Ozawa)   0100

0001, 25th

C. Engano

1140   0600, 25th

Group 'A' (Matsuda)
2000   0822, 25th

2241

Second Striking Force (Shima)   Luzon

Task Force 38 (Halsey's Third Fleet) steams north to engage Ozawa's force

Clark Field

0935 Carrier Princeton hit, sinks at 1630   2345

PHILIPPINE ISLANDS   MANILA   TG 38.3 (Sherman)

Princeton   2000

TG 38.2 (Bogan)

1200, 23 Oct   Mindoro   Sibuyan   San Bernardino Str   0600, 25th

1026/1530 US air strikes. Battleship Musashi sinks at 1935, cruiser Myoko retires damaged   Sea   Masbate

CALAMIAN GROUP   1000 24 Oct   Samar   TG 38.4 (Davison)

1200, 23 Oct   Panay   0400, 25th

Force 'A' (Kurita)   Leyte   US Seventh Fleet (Kinkaid)

0632, 23 Oct US Submarines sink cruisers Atago and Maya, Takao retires damaged   1000 24 Oct   Negros   Cebu   Bohol   Surigao Str

Palawan   2000   2330   TG 38.1 (McCain) to Ulithi

0918 24 Oct   1000

1200, 23 Oct   Force 'C' (Nishimura)   Mindanao

S u l u   S e a

First Striking Force (Kurita)

BRITISH NORTH BORNEO

Sails 22 Oct

BRUNEI

© Richard Natkiel, 1986

into effect, but Toyoda delayed another 36 hours before ordering the elements of the Combined Fleet to move. Catching the invaders in the middle of their landing operations was a vital component of the Japanese plan, but that opportunity seemed to be fading fast.

At noon on the 29th Admiral Kurita's 1st Striking Force reached Brunei Bay, Borneo. Kurita planned to sail his huge fleet of five battleships (including the 64,000-ton monsters *Yamato* and *Musashi*), with their escorts, through the San Bernardino Strait, then turn south to arrive in the middle of the US amphibious force on the 25th. A smaller force of two old battleships would penetrate Leyte Gulf on the same day, having sailed through Surigao Strait. Admiral Shima's 2nd Striking Force, which had now reached Formosa, would transit the Philippines from the north. It would then drive through the Surigao Strait to reinforce the southern pincer – to find it engaged, it was hoped, in the destruction of the American landing forces.

Meanwhile Halsey's powerful fleet had to be neutralized. Simultaneously with these manoeuvres, therefore, Admiral Ozawa's Main Body would sail south from the Inland Sea. It consisted of four carriers, two battleships (converted to launch catapult aircraft), three cruisers and eight destroyers. Yet this was a mere shadow of the once proud Japanese Navy's air arm. There were barely 100 aircraft available, and their pilots were only half trained in the demanding skills of flying from a bucking flight deck in the open ocean.

Ozawa's was a decoy mission – to lure Halsey away from Leyte. Ozawa was ordered to engage and defeat Halsey if he could, but the veteran Japanese admiral himself sanguinely expected 'complete destruction' of his own forces.

Kurita's battleship-heavy force nosed its way into the Sulu Sea east of the Philippines on 22 October. The US submarines *Dace* and *Darter* picked off two heavy cruisers and badly damaged a third. Now Kurita's force, as it pressed on into the Sibuyan Sea, was within range of Halsey's own strike aircraft. But it was the Japanese who launched the first attack from the air. Early on the 24th a large force of Navy bombers, torpedo aircraft and fighters rose from fields on the Philippines to hit the US fleet. Nearly 200 aircraft attempted to fight their way through but, forewarned by radar, Hellcats were already in the air and put up an impenetrable defence. The first wave was met by seven Hellcats from the *Essex*, led by Commander David McCampbell. In less than 30 minutes McCampbell and his wingman, Lt Roy W. Rushing, had shot down 15 Japanese aircraft. Nine

Continued on page 119

A North American B-25J Mitchell of the Royal Netherlands Indies Army Air Corps, based at Darwin, Australia, in 1944.

Curtiss SB2C
Helldivers in
formation, with
Hellcat fighters flying
top cover.

Above. F6F-3 Hellcats aboard USS *Yorktown* in June 1944.

Squadron members triumphantly wave off a bomb-laden A6M from an airbase on the Philippines as it takes off for a one-way Kamikaze mission during the Leyte operations.

A Republic P-47D
Thunderbolt of the US
Army Air Force based
at Saipan in July 1944.

were accounted for by McCampbell, who set a record for one mission in the Pacific war. At the end of only half an hour of aerial combat a third of the Japanese strike force was in the sea. The rest had turned and fled, with Hellcats in hot pursuit almost as far as Manila.

These actions marked the full-scale combat debut of the Japanese Navy's new land-based fighter, the N1K2 Shiden, an exceptional aircraft in the hands of a skilled pilot. The first large unit of Shidens to be pitched against US Navy fighters was the 341 Air Corps, which arrived on Luzon from Formosa on 20 October as part of the Japanese Navy's 2nd Air Fleet. A total of 100 Shidens was attached to this unit but, although they fought well, there were not enough trained pilots to get the best out of this fine aircraft's Hellcat-beating performance. Moreover, they were soon impotent as a fighting force, grounded for lack of spares.

Meanwhile on the morning of the 24th another group of Japanese aircraft had gone after the light carrier *Princeton*, also to be met by a defensive wall of Hellcats. But at 0940 a single Yokosuka D4Y Judy dive-bomber, breaking out of cloud cover, made a shallow run at the ship. Flying through a hail of anti-aircraft fire, the pilot managed to deliver two 500-lb bombs smack on the warship's flight deck. They tore their way through several decks, igniting aviation fuel and exploding six torpedo-armed TBFs. By mid-afternoon the fires had been brought under control, except for a blaze near the stern ammunition stores. At 1530 a great explosion tore open her stern – while flying debris lacerated the topsides of the cruiser *Birmingham* which had drawn alongside, killing over 200 of her crew.

Blazing from end to end, the *Princeton* was abandoned. The Japanese had drawn blood, but Toyoda's air units, whose assignment under the Sho plan was to sweep aside and sink enemy warships

who might block the break-out of the two pincers of the Japanese fleet, had hardly got anywhere near to achieving their mission.

The Japanese Army Air Force had also hurled itself at the invasion force standing off the beachhead. On the 24th it launched mass attacks in an attempt to get through to the warships, but fighters from the escort carriers were quickly ordered to suspend their ground-attack missions to enable them to fend off the strike. Nearly 70 Japanese aircraft, almost half the total number of attackers, fell before US Navy fighters and anti-aircraft guns.

This was the swansong of the Grumman Wildcat. The FM-1 and FM-2 models of the tubby little machine had been kept in production to equip the fighter squadrons of small escort carriers. On 24–25 October FM-1s and FM-2s of VF-76 and from 14 composite squadrons, flying off the 17 escort carriers of Task Group 77, not only provided close air support for the landing, but fended off the strikes on the invasion force. Remaining embarked aboard *Savo Island* after the battle, pilots from VC-27 were credited with the destruction of 62½ Japanese aircraft during four months of operations in Philippine waters, making their squadron the top-scoring escort carrier-based unit.

Meanwhile Admiral Halsey's aircraft had found the Japanese surface warships. A strike on the southern force commanded by Admiral Nishimura failed to achieve much, but the northern force, negotiating the narrow, reef-crowded waters of the Sibuyan Sea, was hit by five massive air strikes. The Americans lost 18 aircraft but the destruction suffered by Nishimura's force was terrible. Helldivers and Avengers hurled bombs and torpedoes at the colossal bulk of the *Musashi*. After receiving 17 bomb and 19 torpedo strikes, the huge battleship rolled over and sank.

Admiral Ozawa's decoy carrier force had now

Continued on page 122

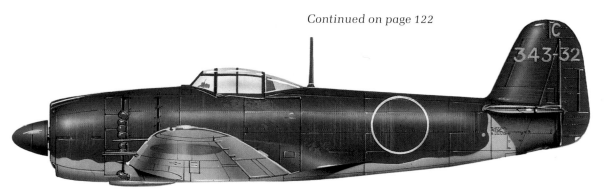

A Kawanishi N1K2-J.
This was a land-based
interceptor fighter,
which first flew in
December 1943.

A detailed view of the
Kawasaki Ki-61 Hien,
a Japanese Army Air
Force fighter of
considerable merit.

A Japanese destroyer blazes after an anti-shipping strike by US Army Air Force B-25s off Leyte.

been brought into the battle. On the morning of the 24th it had launched an air strike on elements of Halsey's 3rd Fleet, but the defenders brushed the attack aside, shooting down half the Japanese planes. The remainder, unable to make carrier landings, flew on to Luzon. Halsey had still to judge the main danger in the three-pronged threat to the Leyte bridgehead. Powerful surface warfare forces were still moving eastwards on two lines of advance but, since Halsey did not know how depleted Ozawa's carrier air groups were, any air threat from the north must have seemed the most menacing. Just before 2000 on the evening of the 24th Halsey ordered the entire 3rd Fleet to move north to engage Ozawa, effectively leaving the San Bernardino Strait wide open for Kurita's force of four battleships and five cruisers to steam through. Ozawa's role as bait in the Sho plan seemed to be working.

During the same night the survivors of Nishimura's Southern Force entered Surigao Strait – where they were smashed to pieces by Admiral Jesse B.

Oldendorf's implacable force of battleships, cruisers and destroyers. But the Northern Force had passed through the San Bernardino Strait during the night, to break out into the Philippine Sea and confront the 7th Fleet's escort carriers and other escort vessels. The main weight of this attack fell on the warships of Rear-Admiral Clifton F. Sprague commanding the northernmost task unit. Quickly Sprague launched his remaining unengaged aircraft, urgently recalling those already on ground-attack missions over Leyte. Running for the cover of a rain squall, he broadcast an urgent plain-language radio call for help.

Japanese shells began to smash into the American vessels. Repeatedly the US destroyers hurled themselves at the heavy enemy warships in order to cover the withdrawal of the vulnerable escort carriers. Sprague's aircraft struck again and again at Kurita's ships, trying to break up their formations. Avengers and Wildcats were armed with anything to hand – bombs, torpedoes, fragmentation bombs, even depth charges. When their bombs had gone, they made strafing runs. When their ammunition had gone they made mast-level passes to confuse the enemy gunners. One pilot, Lt Paul B. Garrison, made 20 strafing runs, ten of them with empty magazines. By 0900 the escort carrier *Gambier Bay* and two destroyers had been sunk. The *Kalinin Bay* had taken 16 shell hits and it seemed that the rest of the fleet would quickly be overwhelmed. Then, at 0911, Kurita broke off the attack, fearful of increasing air attack and anxious to fulfil his primary mission of attacking the bridgehead. Sprague could not believe his good fortune and was convinced that the Japanese were indeed breaking off only by the persistent reports of his ecstatic pilots. At 1230, with the entrance to Leyte Gulf just 50 miles away, Kurita abandoned his attack, swinging round to escape back through San Bernardino Strait.

The attacks on elements of the 7th Fleet that

Far left. The Landing Signals Officer on USS *Lexington* gives a signal with his 'bats' to a pilot coming into land, indicating that one wing is too low.

Above. The US escort carrier *St Lô* blows up following a Kamikaze hit during the Battle of Leyte Gulf, 25 October 1944.

morning were marked by the initiation of a terrible new kind of warfare – the Kamikaze or suicide attack. Volunteer Japanese Navy pilots of Air Groups 201 and 601, together with other Navy units in the Philippines area, had formed the very first Kamikaze (literally 'Divine Wind') squadron. That morning, flying hastily modified Zeros armed with a 550-lb bomb, they made their first one-way missions. The escort carrier *Santee* was struck and set on fire, the *Suwannee* survived a direct hit, but the *St Lô* was not so lucky. She was struck by a Zero, which crashed through the flight deck and exploded ammunition stores, making her the first warship to be sunk by suicide attack.

Meanwhile, Ozawa's carrier force had been found about 200 miles east of Cape Engaño at the northernmost tip of Luzon. From 0815 in the morning of the 25th to late afternoon, strike aircraft from the 3rd Fleet battered the Japanese ships, brushing aside the few fighters that came up to try to protect them. The converted seaplane-carrier *Chitose* was bombed and sunk. The flagship *Zuikaku* was ripped open by a torpedo and Ozawa had to transfer his flag to a cruiser. The *Zuiho* was damaged and the second wave of US aircraft hit the *Chiyoda*. The *Zuikaku*

was struck by three more torpedoes launched by the third strike wave and the last survivor of the carriers that had launched the attack on Pearl Harbor rolled over and sank. The fourth wave found and quickly despatched the already crippled *Zuiho*. The remaining ships would have been crushed by Halsey's battleships, if there had not been an urgent request for help from Admiral Kinkaid, reinforced by a controversial order from Admiral Nimitz, watching the progress of the battle from US Pacific Fleet headquarters in Pearl Harbor. Halsey turned round in pursuit of Kurita, but the danger was evaporating and the fleet had to content itself with catching a lone straggling destroyer. The 3rd Fleet had steamed 600 miles after Ozawa in the north and had then pursued Kurita in the south, but had failed to bring either to a surface battle.

Nevertheless the Battle of Leyte Gulf had put an end to the Japanese fleet as an effective force. The US bridgehead on Leyte was secure and underpinned the reconquest of the whole Philippines. The Japanese lost four carriers, three battleships, including the mighty *Musashi*, six cruisers and 14 destroyers, together with up to 10,000 sailors and many hundreds of the dwindling number of trained pilots.

A Mitsubishi A6M2 based in the Philippines in late 1944.

The crew of the Japanese carrier *Zuikaku* salute as the naval ensign is lowered and the big carrier sinks during the Battle of Leyte Gulf.

RAF Republic Thunderbolt prepared for operations against Japanese ground forces in Burma.

CHAPTER 7

THE RECONQUEST OF
BURMA

The Japanese Threat to India

By March 1942 British forces had effectively been expelled from Burma across the border into India. The next few months saw the Royal Air Force trying to rebuild its shattered strength – waiting for the expected Japanese blow to fall on eastern India itself. In March there were only five squadrons operational; by June there were 26, operating Blenheim IV bombers, Hurricane IIB and IICs fighter and fighter-bombers, and some Vultee Vengeance dive-bombers. The Indian Air Force contributed six Hurricane squadrons and one Vengeance squadron. Although desperately short of resources and manpower, the British theatre commander, Field Marshall Lord Wavell, launched an offensive campaign (the First Arakan) in an ultimately unsuccessful attempt to clear the Japanese from the Mayu peninsula on the Burmese coast. The RAF was heavily engaged, flying both offensive ground-support missions and defending Indian airfields against Japanese counter-strikes.

The 'Chindits', a force of troops trained in jungle warfare, led by the highly unconventional Brigadier Orde Wingate, also began operations behind enemy lines, supported by RAF Dakota air drops. Wingate's first deep-penetration mission began in February 1943 when 3000 men crossed the Chindwin river in northern Burma. They trekked over a 1000-mile trail, doing what damage they could to Japanese lines of communication. Their survival depended entirely on successful resupply from the air, RAF Dakota pilots having to fly low over dense jungle-clad hills at night to find their destination marked by nothing more than flares lit on the ground. The first Chindit operation lasted until the monsoon broke in June.

On 15 November 1943 the unified South East Asia Command (SEAC) was established, embracing all British Commonwealth and American forces in the theatre, with responsibility for operations in Burma, Thailand, Malaya and Singapore and for the defence of Ceylon and the northeast frontier of India. Commanding the air forces was Air Marshal Sir Richard Peirse, with an American deputy, General George Stratemeyer. Their command was divided into a Tactical Air Force under Air Marshal Sir John Baldwin, and a strategic air force commanded by Brigadier General Howard Davidson and a Troop

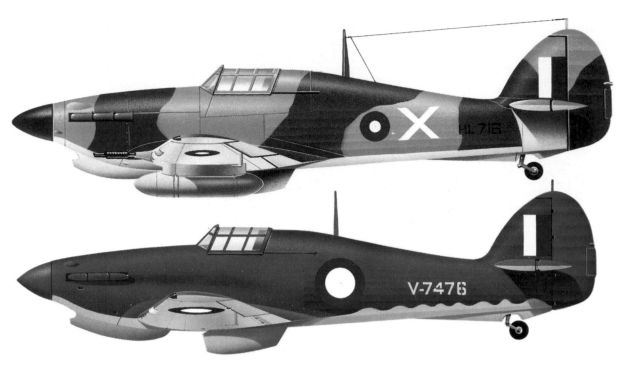

Left and below left. Hurricanes serving with the Indian Air Force and the Royal Australian Air Force respectively. The Hawker Hurricane proved to be one of the most versatile fighter aircraft of World War II.

Carrier Command under Brigadier General D. Old – both US Army Air Force officers. Although the command was not lavishly supplied with the latest aircraft, air strength was building up all the time. Hurricane IICs took on the fighter-bomber role, and Spitfire Vs began arriving in October 1943 and Spitfire VIIIs from early 1944, both aircraft proving superior to the Japanese Army Air Force's primary fighter in the campaign, the Nakajima Ki-44. When SEAC was created, its air force comprised 48 RAF and 17 US squadrons, with a total of 1105 aircraft. There were a further 640 second-line and reserve aircraft in India.

While in the last months of 1943 the Allies were planning to launch a general offensive to recapture Burma, the Japanese moved first, attacking in the south on the Arakan front on 3 February 1944. However, bypassed British and Indian units, supplied from the air, continued fighting and thus cut the Japanese invader's own supply lines. Mitchells, Beaufighters, and Hurricane fighter-bombers made repeated ground-attack sorties against Japanese forces, while Liberator and Wellington bombers carried out long-range strikes on Rangoon and Bangkok. The situation remained critical throughout

February as Allied transport aircraft, including Curtiss C-46 Commandos diverted from operations over the 'Hump' to China, made round-the-clock airdrops to supply the pockets of cut-off British and Indian forces. The Japanese offensive faltered and turned into a retreat, with the British now in pursuit.

On the central front Wingate launched another long-range penetration movement, in which 9000 men and 1000 mules were air-landed by Dakota and by glider behind Japanese lines. At the height of this operation Wingate himself was killed in an air accident, depriving the Chindits of the dynamic personality needed to conduct this kind of irregular warfare in extremely tough conditions. Casualties were very high – some were airlifted out by Sunderland flying boats alighting on Indawagyi Lake. Others were actually flown out on litters by the primitive experimental Sikorsky R4 Hoverfly helicopter.

In the north the US general, 'Vinegar Joe' Stilwell, launched a successful offensive supported by General Claire L. Chennault's 14th Air Force, operating from airbases in China. This in turn led the Japanese to launch an offensive to neutralize US airbases in the Kweilin-Liuchow area, which they eventually

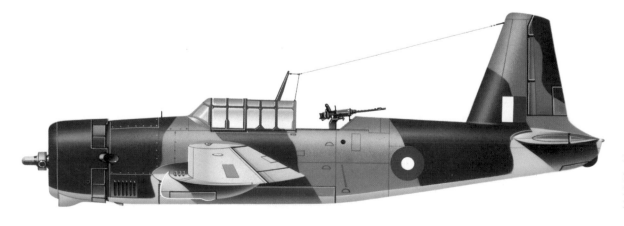

A Vultee V-72 Vengeance dive-bomber used by the RAF for operations in Burma.

Top. A Bristol Blenheim Mk V, escorted by Hurricanes, on a tactical strike mission early in the campaign to reconquer Burma.

Above. Hawker Hurricanes fitted with air-to-ground rockets provided the backbone of the RAF's fighter-bomber strength in the Burma theatre right up to the end of the fighting.

succeeded in overrunning in November 1944.

The Final Japanese Offensive

The major battle for Burma, however, began on 8 March 1944, when the Japanese launched a long-awaited attempt to invade India. Three Japanese divisions spearheaded the attack, but the new tactics that had been devised by General William Slim, commander of 14th Army since October 1943, and used earlier on the Arakan front, were once again successful. By 21 April the Japanese had been fought to a standstill at the Battles of Kohima and Imphal. The British counterattacked, punching through the disintegrating Japanese 15th Army. The most modern and effective aircraft were now reaching SEAC squadrons. P-47 Thunderbolts began to supplant Hurricanes (still the most important British aircraft numerically in the theatre until the end of the war), Mosquitos replaced Vultee Vengeances and Liberators replaced Wellingtons. However the Mosquito, with its wooden airframe bonded with epoxy glues, suffered considerable maintenance problems in the moist, hot tropical climate.

By October the British had crossed the Chindwin river and within a matter of weeks had driven the Japanese from the mountains to the plains, where British armour could be used, as the monsoon rains abated, under a highly protective umbrella of tactical air power. Hurricanes undertook bomber and rocket-firing missions, while Spitfires and Thunderbolts

Continued on page 136

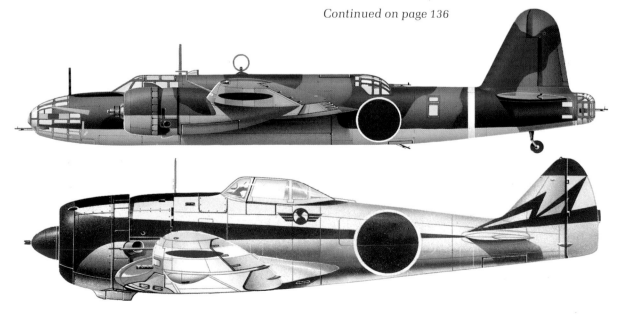

Above right. A Nakajima Ki-49-I based in China in early 1944.

Right. A Nakajima Ki-44-IIb based in Japan in the summer of 1944.

A detailed view of the
Supermarine Spitfire.
This remarkable
aircraft played a
prominent role in the
Burma campaign.

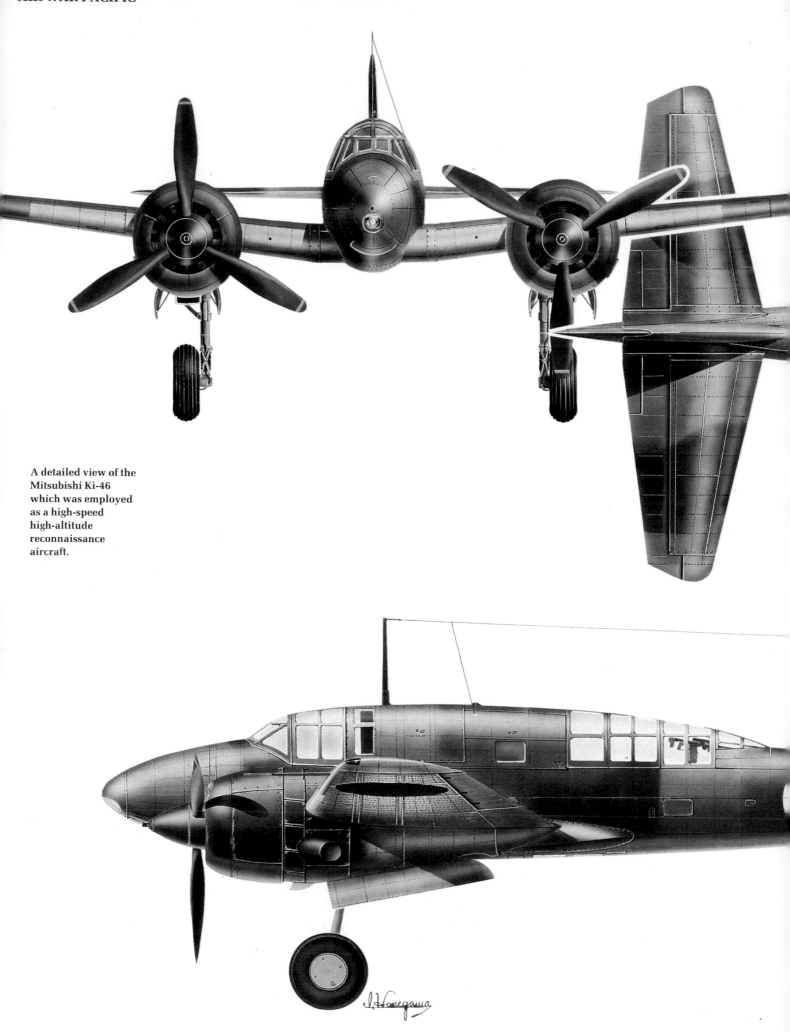

A detailed view of the
Mitsubishi Ki-46
which was employed
as a high-speed
high-altitude
reconnaissance
aircraft.

Left. Deck crews fold the wings of a rocket-carrying Fairey Firefly after a carrier-launched strike on a Japanese oil installation on Sumatra.

Right. Spitfire pilots make their way across a rain-soaked airfield after a sortie against the Japanese.
Below. Spitfires on patrol in the Burma theatre.

Top left. A Spitfire Mk Vc of 54 Squadron, RAF, in Australia in 1943.
Centre left. A Vickers Wellington X of 99 Squadron, RAF, in Burma in mid-1944.
Below left. A Bristol Beaufighter. Supplied to the Royal Australian Air Force, these two-seater strike fighters played havoc with Japanese shipping.

maintained air superiority. Liberator bombers, now escorted by long-range P-51 Mustang fighters, mounted an interdiction campaign against enemy supply lines, hitting railways (including the infamous Bangkok-Moulmein line built by Allied prisoner of war slave labour), stores and supply dumps, ranging deep into enemy territory to strike at ports and shipping in the Andaman Sea and Gulf of Siam. One squadron of Liberators was equipped for minelaying in coastal waters.

Also operating over these waters were dedicated anti-shipping squadrons. Sunderland and Catalina flying boats ranged far over the Indian Ocean, while the Bristol Beaufighter earned itself the grim nickname 'Whispering Death' from the Japanese forces that it flailed with cannon and rocket fire. The twin-engined Beaufighters were particularly effective against river craft, sampans and barges operating along the mangrove swamps and the 'chaungs' or river inlets of the Burmese coastline. By February 1945 they had accounted for more than 700 such vessels. The Royal Australian Air Force, incidentally, made equally effective use of this very potent aircraft, mounting strikes on similar Japanese targets along the coasts of New Guinea, the Celebes and the Philippines.

The Allies Victorious

The Allies began the reconquest of Burma with a three-pronged offensive. In December 1944 a general attack began on the Arakan front. The island of Akyab was captured on 3 January 1945 and Ramree

A Short Sunderland III. This maritime reconnaissance aircraft served with distinction in the southern Pacific region.

Curtiss C-46
Commando, the
backbone of air
transport operations
over the 'Hump' from
India to China.

Below. A de Havilland
Mosquito being towed
into position for a
take-off from the
Cocos Islands in the
Indian Ocean.

island, 70 miles to the south, on 9 February, after an amphibious landing heralded by a smokescreen laid by Hurricanes, and covered by ground-attacking Spitfires, Thunderbolts and Mitchell medium-bomber strikes.

On the central front the British 14th Army advanced on a 140-mile front and captured Meikita on 4 March. Hurricanes operated from jungle airstrips just a few miles behind the front line, using their rockets and cannon to make very effective strikes on Japanese bunkers and on whatever armour remained. In the north US forces were advancing and had reopened land communications with China by the end of January 1945. On 3 May a brilliantly mounted amphibious Allied landing, combined with a parachute drop, led to the recapture of Rangoon. Desperate, last-ditch resistance was offered by fanatical Japanese, but Spitfire and Thunderbolt squadrons, flying ground-attack patrols, ready to be called up by a forward air controller to saturate the jungle with cannon shells and rockets, soon destroyed these last pockets.

In the final clearance of Burma, General Slim's forces accounted for all but 5000 Japanese troops who managed to cross the Sittang river and escape eastwards into Thailand. Victory in this terrible and unforgiving campaign, fought in sweltering malaria-ridden jungle against a fanatical enemy, had depended on air power – not just the fighters that gained air superiority and the ground-attack aircraft that exploited it – but the aircraft of the Combat Cargo Task Force, hauling in supplies from India and then covering many more hundreds of miles to feed and sustain an army of 300,000 men on the ground.

Above right. A
Consolidated
Liberator B Mk VI of
356 Squadron, RAF,
based in the Cocos
Islands, in 1945.
Right. A Nakajima Ki
43-IIb based in Burma.
The type was used in
all areas during the
Pacific war.

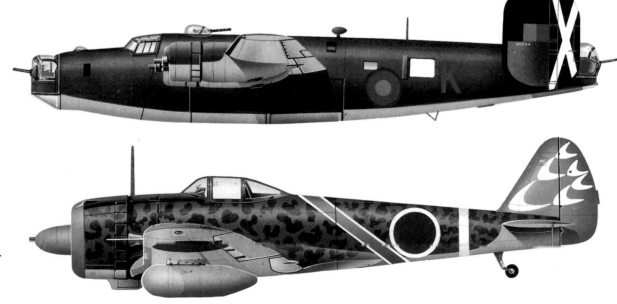

CHAPTER 8

THE LAST BATTLES

Iwo Jima and Okinawa

After the Battle of Leyte, as the US Army Air Force prepared for the strategic bombardment of Japan with the fast-growing fleet of B-29s operating from bases seized in the Marianas, the US Navy could draw breath. But this was only a short respite before its ships, air groups and Marine infantry were pitched once again at the bastions of Japan's 'absolute national defence zone', as American (and now British) air and sea power pressed in on the Japanese home islands themselves.

Land-based naval air power formed the kernel of Japan's air defence strategy. The 1st Air Fleet had

Above. **B25s of the 345th Bombardment Group, the Air Apaches, hit Japanese warships off the China coast in late March 1945.**

moved from the Philippines to Formosa and was slowly rebuilding its shattered units. The 3rd Air Fleet, based on airstrips from Kanto to Kyushu, was responsible for the defence of the Ryukyus. The 11th Air Fleet, based in Kyushu, was ready to beat off any American task force that should try to assault the home islands directly. In February and March two new air fleets, the 3rd and 10th, were created from the survivors of other units. However, because of operational pressures and the lack of fuel for any but the most vital combat missions, training activities were suspended. The numbers of aircraft in front-line service and coming from the factories still looked formidable on paper but their pilots were woefully inexperienced.

Early in 1945 Admiral Raymond Spruance relieved Admiral Halsey as commander of the 3rd Fleet, now renamed the 5th Fleet. As Nimitz's chief of staff, Spruance had in mid-1944 drafted a plan for the seizure of two islands almost at the gates of Japan itself – Okinawa in the Ryukyu chain and Iwo Jima in the Bonins. The capture of Iwo Jima would provide a base for fighter aircraft to escort Tinian-based B-29s in raids on Japan and also an emergency landing site for bombers in trouble on the 2800-mile round trip. The conquest of Iwo Jima, launched on 19 February 1945, was a tough, month-long struggle. Marines fought against fanatical defenders, dug in in volcanic caves. They dubbed one blood-soaked stretch of the Japanese defensive line 'the meat

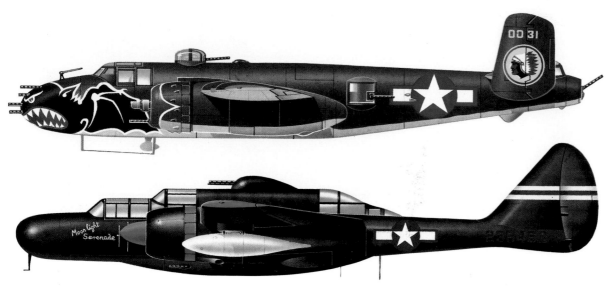

Top left. A North American B25-J Mitchell of the US Army Air Force based in Okinawa in July 1945.
Below left. A Northrop P-61B Black Widow with 550th Night Fighter Squadron, US Army Air Force, in the Philippines in June 1945.

grinder'. The escort carrier *Bismarck Sea* was hit and sunk by suicide aircraft operating from Kyushu on 21 February, the same day on which the fleet carrier *Saratoga* was hit by five Kamikaze Zeros in the space of three minutes. The veteran carrier was now out of the war (she was finally destroyed in the atomic bomb tests at Bikini Atoll in 1946).

By 25 March Iwo Jima was secure. The next target was the 60-mile long, ruggedly mountainous island of Okinawa lying astride Japan's lines of communications with Formosa and the south. In planning to parry the next enemy move the Americans anticipated that the Japanese would concentrate almost all the aircraft available for the defence of Japan itself in the southern island of Kyushu, where they could reach out to attack a force operating in the Ryukyu island chain. Together with aircraft flying from Formosa and from the Chinese mainland, it seemed clear that the Japanese must hurl everything they had at the invasion force.

Nimitz's prime concern was how to counter this threat in the critical period before airstrips could be established on Okinawa itself. Allied carrier forces would have to linger in the combat zone for a long period and within range of up to 4000 land-based enemy aircraft, including Kamikazes.

Meanwhile Task Force 58, with Spruance in strategic and Marc Mitscher in tactical command, had embarked on a pre-invasion softening-up mission to hit airfields in Kyushu and shipping in the Inland Sea. Task Force 58 left Ulithi, the natural

deep-water anchorage in the western Carolines, on March 14. On the 16th it launched attacks on Kyushu airfields, but the Japanese had managed to get most of their aircraft airborne and out of harm's way. After lingering to bomb ground installations, Mitscher's aircraft flew on to hit warships in Kobe and Kure harbours.

That same day the Japanese counterattacked with land-based naval strike aircraft, finding Rear Admiral Radford's group of carriers 75 miles to the south of Shikoku. A bomb hit the *Enterprise* but failed to explode. The *Intrepid* was damaged by a near miss. Three Yokosuka D4Y Judy dive-bombers found and hit the *Yorktown*. One bomb drilled through the signal bridge and exploded below decks leaving two gaping holes in the ship's side.

The next day, 19 March, aircraft from Task Force 58 set out again to hit airfields on Kyushu and warships in the Inland Sea, at the same time inviting another counterattack. The carrier *Wasp* was hit and a bomb penetrated to the mess deck, causing heavy casualties. Two bombs struck the *Essex*-class carrier *Franklin*, which had already survived a Kamikaze attack off Samar in October of the previous year when an aircraft had smashed through her flight deck. Now, once again, she was in grave peril as a single aircraft, which had slipped through the radar pickets, came out of overhanging clouds. One bomb hit the flight deck amidships. The second struck towards the stern and both tore through to the ship's vitals, igniting aviation fuel, bombs and torpedo

Continued on page 145

A Vought F4U-1D Corsair aboard the USS *Essex* in April 1945.

Above. F4Us make a napalm strike on an Okinawa hillside.

Above right. A TBF Avenger drops supplies by parachute to the 1st Marine Regiment, pinned down in the bloody fighting for Shuri Castle on Okinawa, May 1945.

Right. Yokosuka Ohka Model 11, a powered bomb with a 1100kg warhead, found abandoned on Yontan airfield, Okinawa.

A detailed plan of the
Mitsubishi A6M5c.
Less than a hundred of
this type were built.

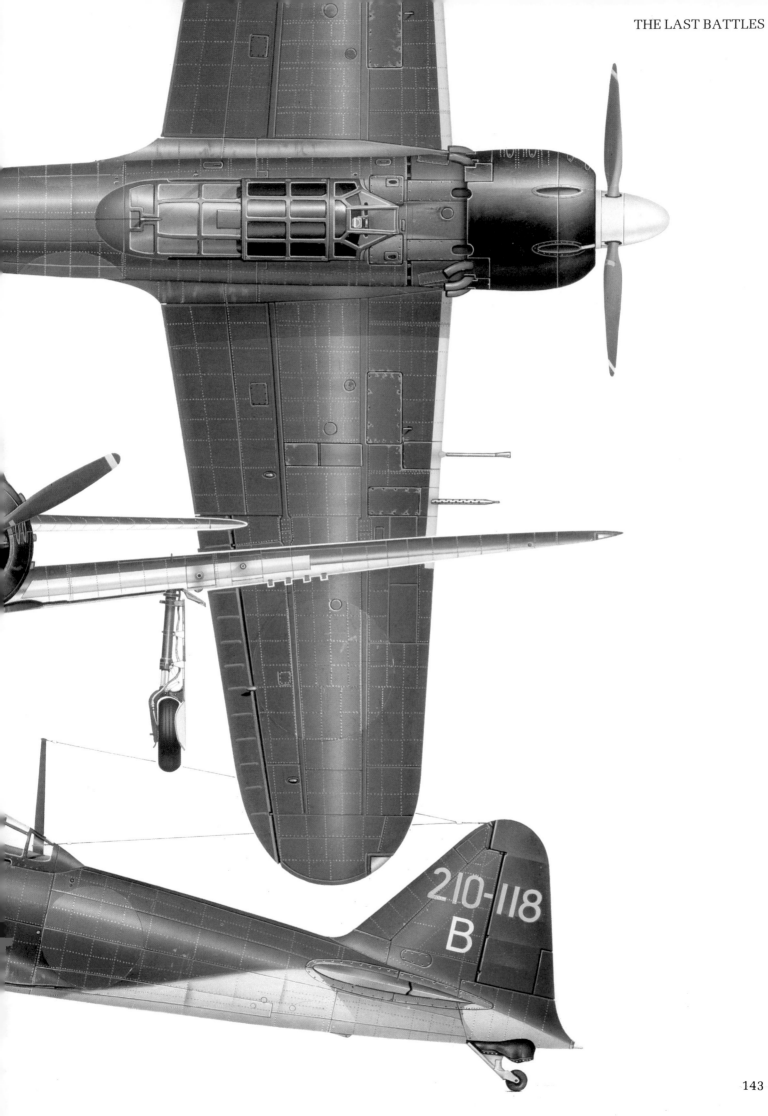

Japanese Navy G4M 'Betty' crews prepare for an Ohka mission. Planned from the start as one-way trips for the Ohka pilot, these missions were also often fatal for the launch crews.

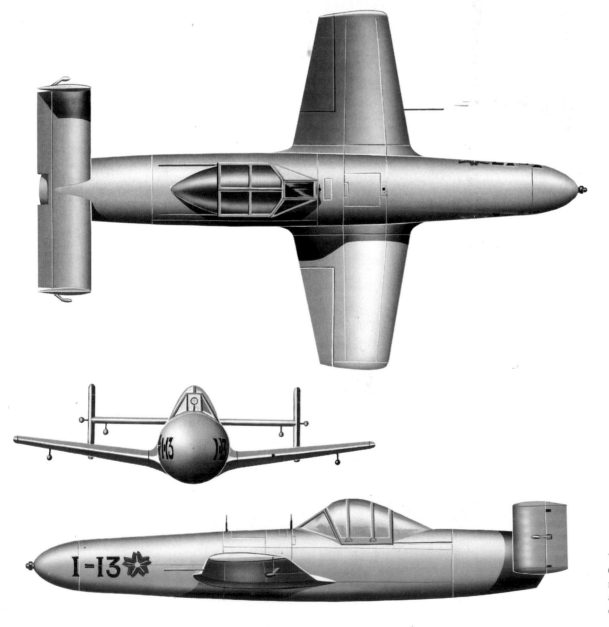

Views of the Yokosuka Ohka 11, which was rocket-propelled with a high-explosive charge in the nose.

Above. **A B-25 passes over a Japanese warship near the China coast.**

warheads. Not quite 50 miles from Japan itself, the big carrier went dead in the water as huge fires blazed within her. Incredibly, showing remarkable bravery the fire-fighting teams got the fires under control and by the early hours of the next morning her crew had restored power. In a great feat of seamanship the charred, battered *Franklin* was sailed to Pearl Harbor and thence to New York for repair. Her casualties, however, were heavy – 764 dead, including her captain, and 260 wounded.

Under this kind of attack Task Force 58 was compelled to pull back, putting up fighter sweeps to try to pin the Japanese down on their Kyushu bases. On the afternoon of 20 March the destroyer *Halsey Powell* was struck by a Kamikaze and severely damaged. A swarm of aircraft attacked the *Enterprise* but were beaten off by intense anti-aircraft fire. The next day a force of G4M Betty bombers, equipped to launch Ohka manned flying bombs, attempted to attack the Task Force but the lumbering mother planes were shot down by a wall of Hellcats before they could launch their stand-off bombs.

In these pre-invasion battles, Task Force 58 pilots claimed the destruction of 528 aircraft both on the ground and in the air. These losses meant that the Japanese were largely powerless to contest the actual

landings when they began on 1 April. On the first day almost 50,000 troops crossed the invasion beaches virtually unopposed.

The Kamikaze Menace

There was, however, something else to hurl against the invaders. This was the Kamikaze squadrons of volunteers who would fly one-way missions in old aircraft packed with explosives and try to take a ship with them in the process.

There had been throughout the course of the Pacific air war 'suicide attacks' by the pilots of blazing and doomed aircraft, steering their crippled planes towards a ship, but there had been no 'official', overtly stated plans for suicide missions until mid-1944. Then the directives for Sho-1, the 'decisive' battle to be fought out in the Philippines, included some suicide operations. The catastrophe and humiliation of the 'Great Marianas Turkey Shoot' which followed, both further depleted the Japanese Navy's supply of trained aircrew and impressed on the survivors a sense of fatalism. They were going to die – but why should they die uselessly?

On 15 October the 50-year-old Rear-Admiral Masafumi Arima, commanding the Manila-based

A Consolidated PB2Y Coronado patrol flying boat of the US Navy, which was designed to replace the PBY Catalina.

26th Air Flotilla, personally led an attack on US warships off Luzon. Intending to die from the outset, he steered his G4M Betty towards a carrier, to be shot into the sea by anti-aircraft fire before he could get near the target. Arima's example was extolled by Admiral Takijiro Onishi, the new commander of the Philippines-based 1st Air Fleet, and the man regarded as the instigator of the Kamikaze idea as a military force. Onishi realized that the only way to counter a US invasion of the islands was a starkly terrifying remedy: aim an old Zero fighter, armed with a 250-kg bomb, at the enemy – one aircraft, one ship.

So-called *Tokko* ('special attack') missions began in earnest on 25 October 1944 – the second day of the Battle of Leyte. A bomb-laden Zero smashed into the American escort carrier *Santee*, ripping open a huge hole in its flight deck. Another Zero hit the *Suwanee*, whose crew managed, like the *Santee*'s, to control the damage. But the escort carrier *St Lô* was not so lucky – a Kamikaze Zero went through the hangar deck, igniting the aviation fuel and starting

calamitous fires that half an hour later blew the ship apart.

Admiral Nimitz called a command conference in late November 1944 to discuss the Kamikaze threat. Significant changes were made to carrier air group composition and the operational practice of fleet air defence – the fighter component of air groups was strengthened. Some compensation for the loss of strike aircraft was gained by modifying F6F Hellcats (and, from December 1944 onwards, F4U Corsairs, at last qualified for carrier operations) as fighter bombers or as platforms for ground-attack rockets. As Kamikaze attacks by night became a growing threat, the *Enterprise* was equipped with 27 radar-carrying Avengers, whose mission was to vector radar-equipped Hellcats into intercept positions.

The composition of task forces was altered to allow for the most effective disposition of anti-aircraft gunfire. In the standard air defence formation, a single large carrier steamed at the centre of a circle with a 2000-yard radius formed by other carriers. Disposed concentrically around them in a

Below. Smoke billows from the USS *Essex*, following a strike by a Kamikaze aircraft on the forward flight deck, November 1944.

Far right. Kamikaze strike on the escort carrier USS *Sangamon.*

circle 4000 yards in diameter were big and small warships – battleships, cruisers and destroyers – bristling with 5-inch dual-purpose, and 40- and 20-mm close-in anti-aircraft weapons. By December 1944 it was clear that this kind of formation was too vulnerable to Kamikaze attack. Destroyers fitted with radar would be stationed up to 60 miles out from the task force to give early warning of an attack and to direct interceptions by the carrier's standing defensive Combat Air Patrols (CAP). These picket ships had their own defensive fighters, 'Jack' patrols, that made low-level sweeps outside the screen, together with CAPs controlled by designated 'Tom Cat' destroyers.

All US carrier aircraft returning from a mission were instructed to circle round the Tom Cats, so that any Kamikazes trying to slip through the screen by tagging along with them could be identified and picked off.

After the initial failure to oppose the Okinawa landing, a great Kamikaze offensive was prepared beginning on 6–7 April. These mass attacks, called *Kikisui* or 'Floating Chrysanthemum', were intended to destroy both the enemy invasion fleet off Okinawa supplying the beachhead and the two mobile carrier task forces providing the umbrella of air power. These were the American Task Force 58, operating between Okinawa and Kyushu, and the British Task Force 57 steaming between Okinawa and Formosa, whose mission was to pin down enemy air power on the southern Ryukyu islands. There was as yet no land-based American air power operable from Okinawa itself.

As the Kamikaze airmen made their ritual preparations for their last mission – and they did so enthusiastically – another one-way mission was setting out. The huge battleship *Yamato* left Kure on the afternoon of 6 April, with only enough fuel to reach Okinawa and without air cover, aiming to bring her 18-inch guns into action against the US transports crowded together off the beachhead.

As the great ship with its destroyer escorts raced southwards, on the afternoon of 6 April, *Kikisui* was put into effect. Wave after wave of aircraft came into attack the invasion fleet. Before the day was over almost 900 planes had taken part, more than a third of them Kamikazes. Three US destroyers were sunk, together with two ammunition ships and one tank-landing ship. The pilots of Task Force 58 claimed to have shot down 249 incoming aircraft.

Continued on page 150

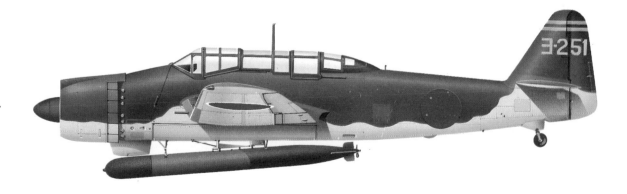

The Aichi B7A2, a Japanese Navy torpedo/dive-bomber. Designed to be launched from a carrier, it only operated in a limited capacity from land bases.

A detailed view of a
Northrop P-61B Black
Widow of the 418th
Night Fighter
Squadron based in the
Pacific theatre.

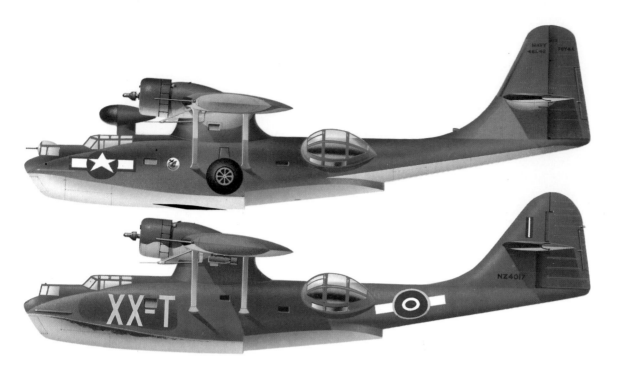

Top left.
A Consolidated
PBY-6A Catalina of
the US Navy.
Below left. A PBY-5 of
the Royal New
Zealand Air Force
based in Fiji towards
the end of the war.

The attacks continued on the 7th. The battleship *Maryland* was hit and two destroyers were damaged. The carrier *Hancock* was struck by a Kamikaze which plunged straight on her flight deck and killed 72 of her crew. However, the damage was contained and the carrier was recovering her aircraft again within two hours.

The *Yamato* Task Group, meanwhile, had been shadowed by US submarines. The battleship was spotted by reconnaissance aircraft from Task Force 58 on the morning of the 7th. At midday 280 US carrier aircraft were launched – Hellcats, Helldivers and Avengers – which pounded the ship and her escorts with a hail of bombs and torpedoes. As the *Yamato* took more and more hits her steering broke down. The wall of anti-aircraft fire from the crippled ship faltered. She was now a wide-open target, dead in the water. At 1423 the *Yamato* turned over and

sank, taking most of her 2400 crew with her. The light cruiser and four destroyers that had accompanied the mighty ship on her death cruise were also sent to the bottom of the East China Sea. Only ten of Task Force 58's aircraft were lost.

Despite the huge depletion of Japanese air power, this was just the beginning of the Okinawa campaign (although there was no surface threat from the Japanese Navy). Throughout April the invasion fleet was pounded daily by anything up to 20 Kamikaze aircraft, together with dive-bombers and torpedo-bombers making conventional attacks. On the 11th there was a second mass attack – 185 Kamikazes, 150 fighters and 45 torpedo-bombers. The attacks were continued the next day and a US destroyer, the *Mannert L. Abele*, became the first victim of an Ohka piloted flying bomb. Although 298 Japanese aircraft were shot down, a battleship and two carriers were

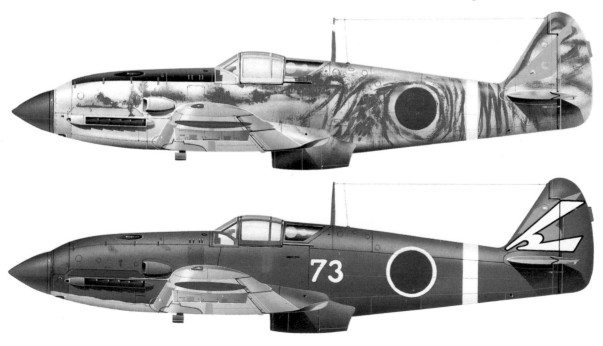

Above left. A
Kawasaki Ki-61-KAIc
based in Okinawa in
1944-5.
Left. A Kawasaki Ki
61-I based in Tokyo
and used in the
defence of the
homeland against US
bomber raids.

A Kawasaki Ki-100-1a. The type was created by fitting a radial engine into the Ki-61 airframe.

damaged. Admiral Nimitz's concern over the Kamikaze threat led him to call for urgent Army Air Force B-29 strikes against the Kyushu air-bases.

On the 16th there was another mass attack – by upwards of 160 aircraft, which smothered the destroyer *Laffey*. Ammunition ships and minesweepers were also sunk. On 28-29 April the fourth *Kikisui* was launched. On the first day two destroyers and three smaller escorts in the outer defensive radar picket screening the beachhead sustained more than ten attacks, but were undamaged. That day six Marine F4U Corsairs fought some 30 Japanese fighters in a ferocious air battle, shooting down 12 and driving off the rest.

The British Contribution

The Royal Navy carriers of Task Force 57 – *Illustrious*, *Victorious* and *Indomitable* – had been engaged in flying off strikes against Sakishima on 16–17 April. The British had been putting a new Pacific fleet together since September 1944. At first this undertaking was met by the American commanders with some trepidation. Admiral King had reluctantly agreed to British operations in the Pacific as long as the Royal Navy could contribute a balanced self-supporting force. There were no American resources to be diverted, and both King and MacArthur were suspicious of British motives as British ships turned up in 'America's' war.

In fact the Fleet Air Arm of 1944 was already very familiar with US naval aircraft and operating techniques. A British fleet carrier operated on average 54 aircraft – typically 38 fighters and 16 Avenger torpedo-bombers, compared with the 80 planes of their US equivalents, but the three-inch armoured flight deck was to prove invaluable off Okinawa. The Seafire remained the Royal Navy's primary indigenous carrier fighter, but the air groups of the British Pacific fleet were now composed largely of American aircraft – Hellcats, Avengers and Corsairs. In fact the Royal Navy made efficient use of the big Corsair as a ship-borne aircraft well before the US Navy did.

British-operated Grumman Hellcat fighters had first gone into action in August 1944 when aircraft from *Indomitable* made strikes on targets in the Netherlands East Indies. These aircraft scored their first air-to-air combat victories during operations over the Nicobar Islands in October, and took part in strikes against Belawan Deli in December. In January 1945 the Royal Navy moved its base from Trincomalee in Ceylon (Sri Lanka) to Sydney, Australia. On the way the carrier squadron, commanded by Admiral Sir Philip Vian, launched strikes against the oil refineries at Palembang in southern Sumatra. On 24 January 43 Avengers, Corsairs, Hellcats and Fairey Fireflies raided the Soengi Gerong refinery, destroying most of the storage tanks and crippling production of this vital source of aviation fuel. An attack on the Pladjoe refinery five days later completely halted production and destroyed nearly 70 Japanese aircraft.

Now the presence of a powerful task force right at the centre of the Okinawa operation was greeted gratefully by the American naval commanders. Task

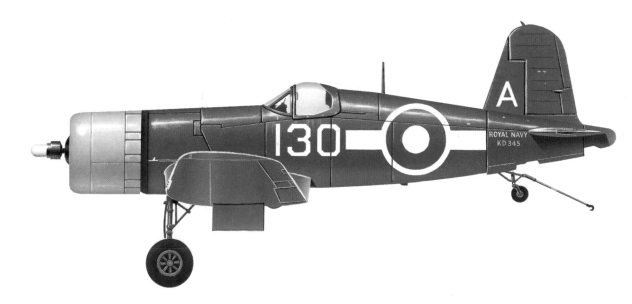

A Vought F4U Corsair IV serving with 1850 Squadron, Royal Navy, in August 1945.

An F6F Hellcat spotted on the deck of the escort carrier USS *Randolph* in May 1945.
Opposite. A Yokosuka D4Y 'Judy' dives flaming into the sea. The few Japanese aircraft that penetrated the fighter cover were met with a wall of fire thrown up by US Navy ships.

Force 57, reinforced by a number of Royal Australian Navy warships, was originally due to return to Leyte on 16 April, but its commander, Admiral Rawlings, offered to stay on station and continue to pin down the southern Ryukyus. Strikes were flown against airfields on Mikayo and Ishigaki islands on the 20th: 19 aircraft were lost but 33 of the enemy were shot down in combat and 38 destroyed on the ground. Task Force 57 set a Royal Navy record by staying at sea for 32 consecutive days.

The first week of May brought no respite for the invasion force. A fifth massed *Kikisui* attack was mounted on 3–4 May and it was the escort ships on the perimeter of the concentric radar picket round the bridgehead that bore the brunt of the Japanese onslaught. Three destroyers and three landing ships were sunk. On 4 May alone 370 US sailors died on picket station duty.

The British, meanwhile, had returned to their position off Sakishima and renewed attacks on airfields on Miyako and Ishigaki islands. Japanese aircraft counterattacked and the carrier *Formidable* was hit by a Kamikaze. On the 9th the *Victorious* was struck and the *Formidable* hit again. It was estimated that the same kind of hits on a US carrier, without an armoured flight deck, would have meant months of repairs at a fleet base.

There was a sixth mass-suicide attack on the 11–13 May, when 250 aircraft severely damaged two picket destroyers and succeeded in breaking through

the defensive combat air patrols to hurl themselves at Mitscher's own flagship, the carrier *Bunker Hill*. Mitscher himself was lucky to escape, as 11 of his own staff were killed. He had to transfer his flag to the carrier *Enterprise*, itself hit by a Kamikaze on the 14th. Again Mitscher had to transfer flags, this time to the carrier *Randolph*.

Two more mass attacks came on 23–25 and 27–29 May, and again two destroyers were sunk – but it was clear by the end of the month that the Japanese counter-offensive was running down. The Japanese simply did not have enough aircraft left to hurl suicidally at the Okinawa bridgehead. It was plain that the American grip could not be loosened and that men and machines would have to be conserved for the now inevitable final battle that would be fought for Japan itself.

By 21 June the land campaign for the island was effectively over. The next day the last *Kikisui* attack was made when defending Hellcats shot down 29 out of 44 attackers, scattering the others before they could engage any warships. Casualties in the Okinawa fighting were higher than in any other Pacific campaign – US Navy deaths, at 4907, exceeded the number of wounded – 4824. The Americans and the British had lost 38 ships, with 368 damaged, and 763 aircraft. But the Japanese had lost 11,000 men, 16 ships and a staggering total of 7800 aircraft – plus, of course, the island of Okinawa itself, just one hour's flying time from Kyushu.

Mitsubishi A6M5 of the Genzan Kokutai, based at Wonsan in North Korea during the winter of 1944. As indicated by the orange undersides, the aircraft was used for training.

B-29s head for North Field on Guam after a city-razing mission over Japan.

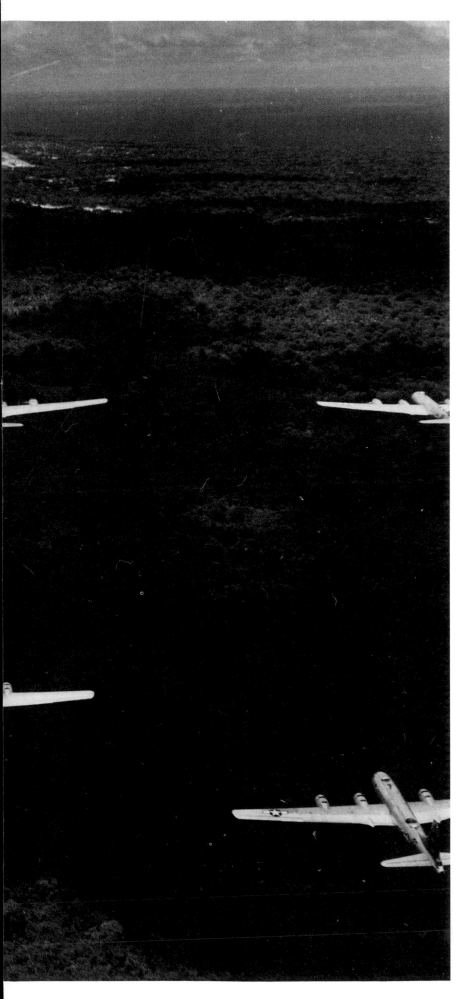

CHAPTER 9

THE STRATEGIC BOMBING OF JAPAN

The Boeing Superfortress

American belief in the power of the strategic bomber to win wars was given powerful reinforcement by the operations of the US 8th Air Force from bases in Britain from 1942 onwards against the industries and cities of Germany.

But Japan's strategic design had pushed out a defensive perimeter which denied American air power an 'unsinkable aircraft carrier' anchored off a hostile continent, from which raids could be mounted. The carrier-launched B-25 'Doolittle' raid on Tokyo in April 1942 had been a brave but unrepeatable experiment. However, the seizure of island bases in the western Pacific and the advent of the Boeing B-29 Superfortress (originally conceived as a 'hemisphere' defence weapon' for intervention in Europe in case bases in Britain should be denied) brought the Japanese home islands themselves under threat.

Bigger, faster, and higher-flying than any bomber before, the B-29 could carry ten tons of bombs almost 6000 miles. The aircraft mounted 12 0.5-inch machine-guns in remote-control barbettes and a 20-mm cannon in the tail. Four 2200hp Wright twin-row radial engines drove the Superfortress at up to 365mph at 25,000 feet. Pressurization of the crew areas gave the aircraft its distinctive cigar tube fuselage, and allowed normal crew operations at 30,000 feet and above.

With American eyes on the plight of the democracies in Europe, initial development contracts were granted in June 1940 and large-scale production was authorized in May 1941 when the US Army Air Force placed orders for 250 aircraft 'off the drawing board'. Pearl Harbor brought a rash of new orders. By the time the prototype XB-29 made its first flight on 21 September 1942, production tooling was in place for no less than 1664 aircraft.

It was a great gamble on General Henry Arnold's behalf. Each B-29 consumed the resources needed to build 11 P-51 Mustangs. The B-29 combined a variety of radical technological innovations – all being tested in a greatly telescoped development

Top left. Stripped of its armament, this B29 Superfortress was used to transport fuel from India to China.

Below left. This Boeing B-29, based on Tinian in the Marianas, was used for the final bombing assault on Japan.

B-29s assume stepped formation soon after their departure from Guam.

Above. B-29s lined up on an airfield.

programme. Data that would normally be derived from prototype testing had to come from wind tunnel and slide rule calculations. There was a design risk in the aircraft's exceptionally high wing loading, but Boeing engineers convinced critics that any increase in wing area would seriously degrade the B-29's performance. Big Fowler flaps, increasing the wing area by 20 per cent, cut the high-wing loading during take-off and landing.

There were severe problems with engine overheating and, initially, with the semi-automated defensive fire system. However, one by one, all the snags were resolved, ensuring that the first pre-production examples of this remarkable aircraft were ready for their crews by 1 June 1943, when the first unit, the 58th Bombardment Wing was set up at Salina, Kansas.

On 7 November 1943 the XX Bomber Command was instituted to control the ever-growing number of VH (Very Heavy) wings training in the American Midwest. It took up to 27 weeks to train a pilot on the big, advanced aircraft, 15 to complete the navigator's training and 12 to qualify an air-gunner. By the end of 1943 only 67 pilots had flown a B-29 and a bare handful of complete 11-man crews had been brought to combat readiness.

Air Bases in China

General Arnold had originally proposed deploying B-29s to Chengtu in south-central China in order to bring southern Japan within range. Chengtu would have to be supplied by air over the 1000-mile 'Hump' of the Himalayas, and offensive operations would mean long over-flights above the Japanese-held mainland. It was not until May 1944 that Brigadier-General Kenneth B. Wolfe, commanding XX Bomber Command, established his headquarters and a clutch of staging bases near Calcutta, India, while forward bases near Chengtu were being prepared by an army of Chinese labourers.

Before the B-29s could mount any missions from China, however, they had to join the airlift of fuel and supplies over the Hump. Known with grim humour by the pilots that flew it as the 'Aluminium Trail' because of the number of crashed aircraft that dotted the route, the Hump was the air route from British India to China, passing over the Japanese-held land route – the Burma Road. From airfields in the Brahmaputra valley across the towering peaks of the Himalayas to Kunming in Yunnan province, the route was some 550 miles long and aircraft had to negotiate a series of 10–14,000-foot mountain ranges. The Hump itself was the 15,000-foot Satsung Range between the Salween and Mekong rivers.

The first missions over the Hump were flown in April 1942 by fuel-laden US Army Air Force Douglas C-47s. As the tempo of operations mounted, bigger aircraft came on to the scene – Curtiss C-46 Commandos, Douglas C-54s, and C-87 and C-109 tankers. By 1945 the Hump was averaging 45,000 tons of supplies per month compared with a grand total of 650,000 tons in 1942–45.

On arrival in India, in preparation for getting a strategic bombing force in place on the other side of the Hump, some of the newly deployed B-29s were stripped of all combat equipment and provisioned as flying tankers. This essential transport role *Continued on page 164*

Continued on page 164

A detailed view of the
B-29 Superfortress,
which wrought such
devastation on
Japanese cities.

44

THE BIG STICK

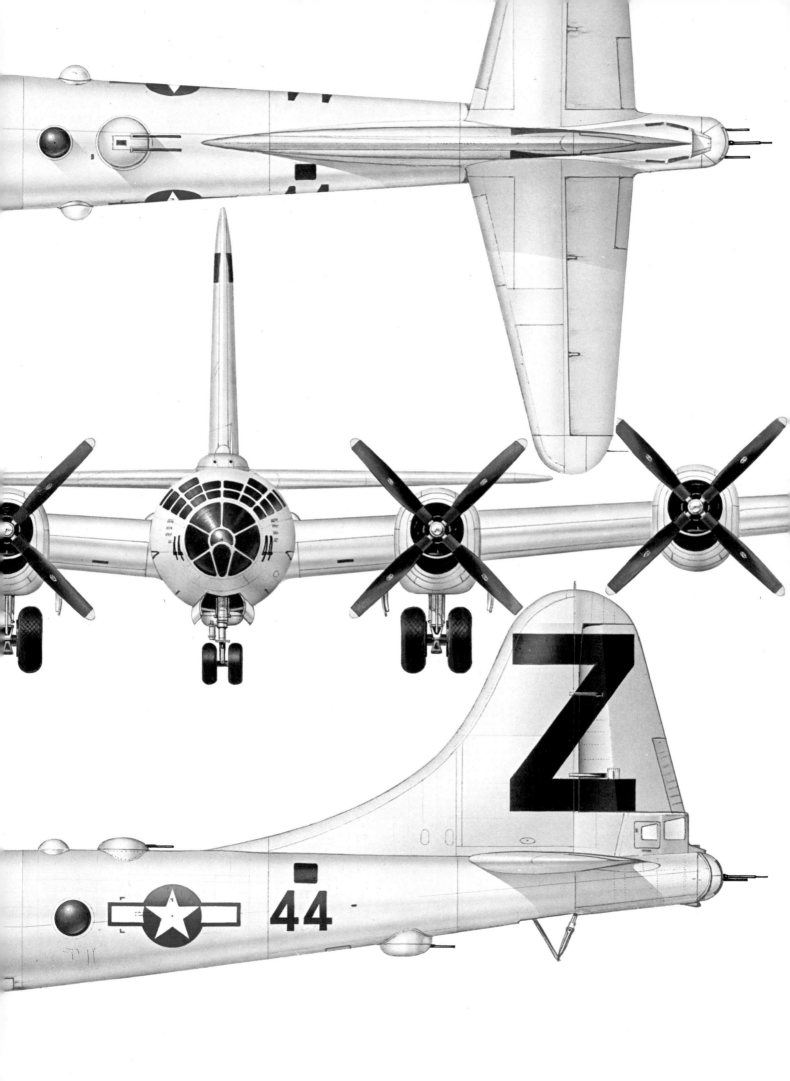

The sheer hitting power of the B-29 is demonstrated by the pattern of bomb craters plastering a Japanese city's railway yards.

interfered with the operational training schedule and, when the first combat mission was planned, the majority of the 240 crews in XX Bomber Command had an average of only two hours' training on the complex new aircraft.

A short, intensive training period was consequently instigated before the B-29s were committed to their first mission, an attack in daylight on the Makasan marshalling yards in Bangkok, Thailand. A 100 aircraft took off from bases in India to make the raid, on 5 June 1944. A heavy overcast sky obscured the target, so the attack was made from high altitude using AN/APQ-13 ground-mapping, navigation and attack radar, derived from the British H$_2$S system. The debut of the wonder weapons was not a great success. Only 18 bombs fell within the target area. Five aircraft crashed on landing and 42 more put down on scattered airfields as they ran out of fuel.

Nine days later, on June 14, 68 B-29s, flying from Chengtu, attacked Japan itself, attempting to hit a steelworks at Yawata on Kyushu island by night. Once again the mission was an almost complete failure. Six aircraft were lost in accidents and one fell to enemy action.

For two months the campaign continued fitfully, the B-29s attacking targets on Kyushu, and in Manchuria and Borneo. Wolfe was recalled to the United States to work on the B-29 engineering programme and replaced by Brigadier General LaVerne Saunders, who took over until September 1944 when Major General Curtis E. LeMay arrived. In November 1944 the XXI Bomber Command, led by

Brigadier General Haywood Hansell, was activated, ready to go into action from bases in the newly captured Marianas Islands, Guam, Tinian and Saipan, where five huge airfields were constructed, each accommodating a wing of 180 B-29s and 12,000 men under the operational command of the newly formed XX Air Force.

LeMay, meanwhile, was doing what he could to galvanize the China-based bombers into an effective force. Night operations were abandoned. Attacks would be made in daylight led by experienced target

Below. A line-up of P-51 Mustangs of the US Army Air Force.

A Mitsubishi J2M
Raiden, which took
part in the defence of
the Japanese
mainland in 1945.

marker crews. LeMay determined that the actual bombing run could be controlled both by the bombardier and the radar operator, so whoever had sight of the target at the release point could trigger 'bombs gone'. Results came slowly but they were improving – aircraft factories on Kyushu were hit on 25 October and another aircraft production target in Manchuria on 7 December, but the difficulties of supplying Chengtu denied LeMay the chance to get the concentration of force and mount the kind of mass bombing attacks he had prosecuted to such effect over Germany with the 8th Air Force. Chengtu itself was within range of Japanese air attacks and stiffening air defences were claiming more and more aircraft. When these losses were added to those in landing accidents, 147 aircraft had been lost by the end of 1944. The offensive was faltering.

At the end of the year, with the huge Marianas bases now operational, it was decided to run down the China-based B-29 operations. The last mission, flown against targets in Formosa to divert attention from the landings in Luzon, took place on 15 January, 1945. Meanwhile the tempo of island-based operations was accelerating fast. Target priority had been switched from steel plants to airframe and aero-engine production centres. They were, it was

Below. Huge airfields
were created on the
Marianas Islands,
with many thousands
of ground crew and
logistics personnel to
support the B-29
operations against the
Japanese home
islands.

planned, to be destroyed, one by one, by high-altitude precision bombing in daylight. However, a series of 'shakedown' raids in the last months of 1944 revealed serious problems with the strategy. Bomb loads had to be cut to permit acceptable performance at high altitude, and engines overheated and failed because of the prolonged climbs required at high gross weights. Bombing accuracy, too, was very poor. The newly trained B-29 crews had few skills in maintaining high-level formations, and blind bombing using radar through cloud proved disappointing.

On 24 November a force of 11 B-29s was flying from Saipan to attack the Nakajima plant at Musashi in the Tokyo prefecture, a vitally important supply centre of aero-engines. As the bombing force approached the coastline of Honshu at altitudes of 27–32,000 feet it flew straight into the westerly-blowing jet stream, the very strong high-altitude wind at the edge of the stratosphere. The winds blew the B-29 formations apart. Those aircraft that got near the target area dropped their bombs at random through cloud. This and ten more raids on the Musashi plant did minimal damage, for the loss of 40 aircraft, each with an 11-man crew.

The Mass Bombing Raids on Japanese Cities

Daylight precision bombing of strategic economic targets was not working. At the end of January the pugnacious LeMay was switched to lead the XXI Bomber Command with new tactics and new targets. The B-29s would now go for area attacks on Japanese cities, dropping incendiary bombs on their largely wooden centres and burning them out one by one. LeMay ordered these new tactics on 19 February. Over the next two weeks they were tested in raids on Tokyo which destroyed an estimated 30,000 buildings.

High-altitude bombing was abandoned. Henceforth, attacks would be made at night at low level and, because of the minimal night fighter opposition, the B-29s could be stripped of their defensive armament (except for the tail-gun) to enable them to take an even bigger bombload. Each B-29 could carry 24 500-lb clusters of M69 incendiaries, containing an unextinguishable mix of jellied petrol, oil, magnesium powder and sodium nitrate, distributed in a pattern of 8,333 bomblets per square mile.

The first low-level night attack was made against Tokyo on the night of 9-10 March by 325 B-29s led by pathfinder crews. In two hours the 279 aircraft which arrived over the target burned out the entire

Left. Hiroshima six months after the atomic attack of 6 August 1945 had killed 100,000 people.

heart of the old city. Some 84,000 people perished. Only 14 B-29s were lost.

Nagoya was incinerated on 11–12 March. Osaka, Kobe and Nagoya were laid waste over the next few nights. During April Tokyo, Kawasaki and Yokohama were hit as the number of available aircraft rose to 500.

Soon after the first B-29 raids the Japanese armaments industries put into effect plans to disperse production to underground sites. Aircraft manufacture had priority but it was April before the mass disassembly of factories and their resiting in abandoned quarries, textile mills, tunnels and even department store basements had begun in earnest – and by then it was too late. By the time of surrender there was scarcely a village that did not have some sort of aircraft manufacturing activity going on. Meanwhile over 100 underground final assembly factories were in various stages of completion, but not yet ready for use. Production was, however, dropping – from a peak of 2572 aircraft completed in the month of September 1944 to 1131 aircraft in July 1945.

The ability of Japanese night fighters, equipped with primitive radar, to intercept the nightly bomber streams was slight, although 43 B-29s were lost out of 464 which bombed Tokyo on 25 May.

Troubled by the losses on this raid, LeMay now sought to engage the defending Japanese fighters with long-range P-51 Mustang escorts flying from Okinawa. On 29 May 454 B-29s appeared over Yokohama in daylight. In the air battles that followed 26 Japanese fighters were shot down for the loss of four B-29s and three P-51s. But the Japanese air defence was faltering. Starved of fuel and spare parts, its aircraft were being drawn into last-ditch Kamikaze attacks.

With Japan's major cities reduced to charred wastelands, the B-29s roamed at will, hitting smaller cities and towns. The programme began on 17 June with attacks on Kagashima, Omuta, Hammatsu and Yokkaichi, 57 cities being devastated in these secondary raids. In addition, during 1945 Pacific-based B-29s flew 1528 minelaying sorties in the waters around Japan, planting by parachute more than 12,000 mines – which were estimated to have sunk 800,000 tons of Japanese shipping.

After four months of saturation bombing Japan had hardly any targets left worth attacking. There were, however, two – the cities of Hiroshima and Nagasaki – targets respectively for atomic weapons delivered by B-29s on 6 and 9 August 1945. The Emperor announced Japan's surrender on 15 August. The war in the Pacific – and the war in the air – were over.

Opposite The atomic bomb missions against the cities of Hiroshima and Nagasaki on 6 and 9 August 1945 were the climax of the Pacific air war – and the beginning of a totally new era in human conflict.

Below. The Japanese delegation sign the formal surrender aboard the battleship USS *Missouri* anchored in Tokyo Bay.

A Consolidated B-24J-190 Liberator of the 43rd Bomb Group. Liberators took part in the final bombing assault on Japan.

AIRCRAFT PROFILES

Fighter, bomber and reconnaissance aircraft which took part in the Pacific war

Allied Aircraft

Bell P-39 Airacobra

Displaying a highly unconventional design for a single-seat fighter, the P-39 had its engine located behind the cockpit, driving a propeller via a long shaft through which a 37-mm cannon fired. A failure as an interceptor, the type was an effective ground attacker and was employed by USAAF units in New Guinea and during the Guadalcanal campaign.

Crew 1
Power plant Allison V-1710-85, 1200hp
Armament 37 mm cannon, 4 x 0.50-in machine guns
Maximum speed 376 mph
Range 675 miles

Boeing B-17 Flying Fortress

Most of the small force of the USAAF's Pacific-based B-17 Cs, Ds and Es were lost in the opening weeks of the Pacific air war. But even when replacement E-models arrived the four-engined bomber failed to fulfil the high hopes placed in it as a long-range, anti-shipping aircraft. It might just manage to evade Zero fighters at high altitude but its bombing proved completely ineffective against manoeuvring warship targets, and serviceability was a big problem on improvised island airstrips. B-17s flew at Midway but had no impact on the battle. They played a more effective part in the Guadalcanal fighting but in late 1942 the decision was taken to phase the B-17 out of the Pacific theatre.

B-17C
Crew 9
Power plant 4 x Wright R-1820-65 radials
Armament 6 x 0.50-in machine-guns,
1 x 0.30-in machine-gun, 10,500lb of bombs
Maximum speed 291 mph
Range 2400 miles

Boeing B-29 Superfortress

A decisive weapon in the Pacific war, the B-29 strategic bomber was ordered off the drawing board in mid-1941. The prototype XB-29 made its first flight on 21 September, 1942 as the result of a huge technical and design effort to create a very large strategic bomber combining a host of technical innovations—all being proven in a greatly telescoped development programme. The weight of the B-29, over 100,000lb. combined with a wing area not much greater than that of a B-17, gave the big aircraft the landing characteristics of a brick – alleviated by the incorporation of large Fowler flaps in the wings that, when activated, increased wing area by 20 per cent.

There were severe problems with engine overheating and, initially, with the semi-automated defensive fire system but, nevertheless, the pre-production examples of this remarkable aircraft were ready for their crews by 1 June 1943 when the first unit was activated. Operations against Japan were put under way in mid-1944 but big strikes began in earnest only in early 1945, launched from island bases in the Marianas.

Conventional bombing raids by B-29s destroyed Japan's cities one by one, and in August 1945 the B-29 became history's only operational atomic weapon delivery system. While 414 B-29s were lost, 147 attributable to enemy anti-aircraft fire and fighter action, B-29 gunners were credited with shooting down 1128 Japanese aircraft.

Crew 11
Power plant 4 x Wright Cyclone R-3350 turbocharged radials, 2200hp
Armament 12 x 0.50-in machine-guns, 1 x 20-mm cannon, 20,000lb of bombs
Maximum speed 357 mph
Range 2650 miles

Brewster F2A Buffalo

Significant as the US Navy's first monoplane fighter, the barrel-fuselaged Buffalo equipped US Navy, US Marine, Netherlands East Indies and RAF units in the opening months of the Pacific war but, woefully outclassed in combat with Japanese Zeros, was withdrawn as soon as it could be replaced by more effective aircraft.

Crew 1
Power plant Wright R-1820-40 radial, 1200 hp
Armament 4 x 0.50-in machine-guns
Maximum speed 321 mph
Range 1000 miles

Bristol Beaufighter (Britain)

This very effective aircraft made its first contribution to the war in 1940 as a night fighter. In the Pacific air war it excelled as a ground-attack and anti-shipping aircraft armed with bombs and rockets, and with a nose bristling with cannon. In the Burma campaign it earned the nickname 'Whistling Death.' The type was built in Australia from mid-1944, equipping Royal Australian Air Force squadrons which wreaked havoc among Japanese shipping along the coasts of New Guinea, the Celebes and the Philippines.

Mk X
Crew 2
Power plant 2 x Bristol Hercules XV11 radials, 1725hp
Armament 4 x 20-mm cannon, 7 x 0.303-in machine-guns
Maximum speed 320 mph
Range 1750 miles

Bristol Blenheim (Britain)

Malaya-based Blenheim light bombers had a very rough handling in the opening months of the Japanese offensive. Later marks, Blenheim Mks IV and V, operated in Burma with some success during 1943-44.

Mk IV
Crew 3
Power plant 2 x Bristol Mercury XV radials, 995hp
Armament 5 x 0.303-in machine-guns, 1000lb of bombs
Maximum speed 266 mph
Range 1460 miles

Chance-Vought F4U Corsair

Designed as a high-performance carrier fighter, the prototype of this distinctive gull-winged aircraft first flew in May 1940. The cranked wing was incorporated in the design to give enough ground clearance for a large, four-bladed propeller to soak up the power of the biggest practicable engine, without excessively long undercarriage legs. The US Navy was at first reluctant to approve the aircraft for carrier operations. The first F4U-1s went to war on Guadalcanal as Marine land-based fighters, a role in which they were to excel in the Pacific air war. The Fleet Air Arm made good use of them at sea, however, and from late 1944 onwards the Corsair flew from US carriers after a decision that carrier air groups should be made fighter-heavy and equipped with the highest-performance aircraft to counter the Kamikaze menace. Goodyear built the aircraft under the designation FG-1.

F4U-5
Crew 1
Power plant Wright 2300hp R-2800-W radial, 2300hp
Armament 4 x 20-mm cannon, 2000lb of bombs
Maximum speed 470 mph
Range 1120 miles

Commonwealth Boomerang (Australia)

Derived from the Wirraway trainer, itself derived from the North American NA33, the Boomerang was an improvised single-seat fighter, rushed into production after the outbreak of the Pacific war. Although they were outclassed by Japanese fighters, 250 were built between 1942 and 1944, seeing service with Australian forces in New Guinea in the fighter, ground-attack and reconnaissance roles.

Crew 1
Power plant Pratt & Whitney R-1830 Twin Wasp, 1200hp
Armament 2 x 20-mm cannon, 4 x 0.303-in machine-guns, 500lb bomb
Maximum speed 296 mph
Range 930 miles

Consolidated PBY Catalina

The most famous flying-boat/amphibian of its generation, the cumbersome-looking PBY had a material effect on the Pacific war at several crucial junctures. Its long range and endurance enabled it to serve the US Pacific Fleet well as a reconnaissance aircraft and fleet shadower. First entering service in 1937, PBY squadrons were badly mauled during the opening Japanese attacks on Oahu and the Philippines, but production of steadily improved versions continued throughout the war. PBYs also served with the RAF, RAAF, RNZAF and the Netherlands East Indies Air Arm. The PBY-5A model of 1942 introduced retractable tricycle landing gear built into the hull.

PBY-5A
Crew 5
Power plant 2 x Pratt & Whitney R-1830-92 radials
Armament 3 x 0.30-in machine-guns, 2 x 0.50-in machine-guns, 4000lb of bombs
Maximum speed 175 mph
Range 2350 miles

Consolidated B-24 Liberator

In essence a mass-produceable bomb-truck, ordered by the USAAF as a back-up to the B-17, the Liberator introduced some radical new design features when it first flew at the end of 1939. Progressively upgraded with better crew protection and heavier defensive armament, the B-24 arrived in the Pacific theatre in January 1942. Its role thenceforth was primarily theatre-tactical, raiding enemy airfields, ports and supply lines as part of combined land-sea-air operations. Other raids were launched at by-passed bastions such as Truk, while Australia-based B-24s made raids on oil installations in Borneo. At peak unit strength there were 11½ USAAF Bombardment Groups in the Pacific equipped with B-24s, divided among seven air forces covering an area of operations of 16 million square miles. The US Navy operated the type as the PB4Y-1 patrol bomber.
First flown in September 1943, the Consolidated PB4Y-2 Privateer was an extensive redesign of the Liberator bomber (evidenced by single fin and rudder, and extended nose) as a specialized, overwater long-range patrol bomber.
A transport version of the Liberator, designated C-87, could accommodate 25 passengers with a crew of five.

B-24D
Crew 10
Power plant 4 x Pratt & Whitney R-1830-65 radials, 1200hp
Armament 10 x 0.50-in machine-guns, 8800lb of bombs
Maximum speed 303 mph
Range 2850 miles

Consolidated B-32 Dominator

It was designed as a lower-technology risk back-up to the B-29 programme, but a long development period meant that only 15 examples of this large, shoulder-wing bomber reached the Pacific in time to see operations against the Japanese.

Crew 10
Power plant 4 x Wright R-3350-23, 2200hp
Armament 10 x 0.50-in machine-guns

Maximum speed 320 mph
Range 3000 miles

Curtiss C-46 Commando

Bigger and more capacious than its great contemporary, the C-47, the Commando was based on a prewar design for a pressurized commercial transport. Operated as a troop and cargo transport by the USAAF, US Navy and Marine Corps, the aircraft could accommodate 40 fully equipped troops. C-46s provided the backbone of the 'Hump' airlift from India to China over the Himalayas.

Crew 3
Power plant 2 x Pratt & Whitney R-2800-51, 2000hp
Armament none
Maximum speed 195 mph
Range 1170 miles

Curtiss P-40 Warhawk

A development of the radial-engined P-36 of mid-1930s vintage, the P-40 was ordered by the US Army Air Corps in 1939 as its standard, single-seat pursuit aircraft. Large numbers were caught and destroyed on the ground in the opening Japanese strikes on Oahu and the Philippines. In Hawaii every single fighter was destroyed in the first Japanese attack, including 62 P-40Bs and 11 P-40Cs.
In China the aircraft fared much better: 100 P-40Bs equipped the American Volunteer Groups (the Flying Tigers) from mid-1941 onwards. The AVG Commander, Claire L. Chennault, taught his pilots to use the P-40s' ruggedness and diving ability to outfight the nimbler, faster-turning Zero. From their inception until 12 July, 1942, when they were absorbed by the USAAF, the Flying Tigers were officially credited with the destruction of 286 Japanese aircraft – for the loss of eight pilots killed in action and four missing. The top-scoring AVG P-40 ace, Robert H Neale, was credited with 16 air combat victories, while eight more P-40 pilots scored ten or more kills.
But, despite its long production run through many upgraded models, the P-40 was not a popular aircraft with pilots. It performed poorly at high altitude and was more successful as a ground attacker than as a dogfighter. The lightweight P-40N was the fastest of the line, attaining 378 mph at 10,500 feet, and the most widely built – performing most of its operational service in the Pacific in ground-attack and escort roles. Production ceased in December 1944.

P-40B
Crew 1
Power plant Allison V-1710-73 in-line, 1150hp
Armament 2 x 0.50-in machine guns, 2 x 0.30-in machine-guns
Maximum speed 352 mph
Range 730 miles

Curtiss SB2C Helldiver

Designed as a carrier-borne replacement for the SBD Dauntless dive-bomber, the Helldiver suffered from design constraints imposed by the requirement that two of the aircraft should fit standard US Navy carrier

elevators. The truncated barrel-like fuselage resulted and problems with lateral stability demanded many design fixes before the type finally became operational in the Pacific in November 1943.
A non-naval variant was designed for the USAAF as the A-25. Most were assigned to Marine Corps squadrons as ground-attack aircraft.

SB2C-3
Crew 2
Power plant Wright R-2600-20, 1900hp
Armament 5 x 0.50-in machine guns, 2000lb of bombs
Maximum speed 294 mph
Range 1925 miles

De Havilland Mosquito (Britain)

This famous wooden-airframe, high-speed aircraft served extensively in the Pacific and Burma theatres with RAF and RAAF squadrons in the fighter, bomber and reconnaissance roles. In the closing stages of the Pacific War, an experimental variant was considered, armed with two 'Highball' bouncing bombs for anti-shipping attacks.

PR 34
Crew 2
Power plant 2 x Rolls Royce Merlin 76, 1710hp
Maximum speed 425 mph
Range 3500 miles

Douglas TBD-1 Devastator

Famous in the first months of the Pacific War for the bravery of its crews if not for its effectiveness as a warplane, the TBD was the US Navy's standard carrier-borne torpedo-bomber from 1937. Slow and lumbering and armed with just a single forward-firing and one rear-mounted machine-gun, the Devastator proved terribly vulnerable in its opening encounters at the Battle of Coral Sea and Midway.
The 'Slaughter of the Devastators' at Midway was the type's last front-line action.

Crew 2
Power plant 1 x Pratt & Whitney R-1830-64 Twin Wasp, 900hp
Armament 2 x 0.30-in machine-guns, 1000-lb bomb or torpedo
Maximum speed 206 mph
Range 716 miles

Douglas SBD Dauntless

The Douglas SBD Dauntless, variously known to its crews as the 'Barge' or the 'Speedy D', was not the most modern warplane when it first saw combat at the outset of the Pacific war, but its outstanding feature was its ability to provide a rock-solid platform in a steep dive for the pilot to release bombs accurately. Although draughty and noisy and notoriously tiring to fly in long, over-water flights, the machine was forgiving in battle. The SBD's airframe was built to take high stress and pilots could throw it around aggressively, pulling up to nine-g without breaking the machine apart. Dauntless pilots proved decisive at the Battles of Coral Sea and Midway and were extensively engaged in the Solomon Islands campaign. The USAAF operated the type as the A-26, and a total of 5936 were built until production ceased with the SBD-6 in 1944.

SBD-5
Crew 2
Power plant Wright R-1820-60 radial, 1200hp
Armament 2 x 0.50-in machine-guns, 2 x 0.30-in machine-guns, 1200lb of bombs
Maximum speed 255 mph
Range 1115 miles

Douglas C-47
Called the Skytrain by the USAAF and the Dakota by the RAF, the C-47 was a military version of the DC-3 civil transport – and proved to be one of the most important Allied aircraft of the war. It delivered paratroops, hauled cargo and towed gliders all over the Pacific and China-Burma-India theatres. The C-47B had engines fitted with high-altitude superchargers and carried extra fuel for the dangerous flight over the Hump across the Himalayas from India to Chiina.
A copy of the DC-3, based on a pre-war licence deal, was built for the Japanese Navy by Nakajima and Showa as the L2D. Named 'Tabby' by the Allies, Japanese-build DC-3s were met throughout the Pacific theatre and often led to disastrous recognition errors.

Crew 2 + 27 troops
Power plant 2 x Pratt & Whitney R-1830 radials, 1200hp
Maximum speed 230 mph
Range 1600 miles

Douglas C-54 Skymaster
The USAAF commandeered the Douglas production line of DC-4A long-range civil transports in 1942 and almost 1000 of these big, robust aircraft were built in the war years, operating across the Himalayas and the Indian Ocean, and establishing long-range air links from the US west coast to Australia and the southwest Pacific.

Crew 3
Power plant 4 x Pratt & Whitney R-2000 radials, 1450hp
Maximum speed 227 mph
Range 2500 miles

Douglas A-20 Havoc
Originally developed in 1939 as a private venture, the A-20 served with the RAF, the USAAF, the US Navy and the Soviet Air Force. USAAF A-20 Havocs were used extensively in the southwest Pacific as attack bombers and anti-shipping aircraft. The A-20G had the bombardier's glazed forward fuselage replaced with an 'attack nose' bristling with cannon or machine-guns. A night fighter version, designated P-70, also served in the Pacific until replaced by the Northrop P-61 in late 1944.

Crew 3
Power plant 2 x Wright R-2600-11 radials, 1600hp
Armament 8 x 0.3-in machine-guns, 4000lb of bombs
Maximum speed 317 mph
Range 1025 miles

Fairey Fulmar (Britain)
This two-seater carrier fighter was in operation in the Indian Ocean in April 1942, successfully fending off the attacks of Admiral Nagumo's carriers on Colombo and Trincomalee.

Crew 2
Power plant 1 x Rolls Royce Merlin VIII
Armament 8 x 0.303-in machine-guns, 500lb of bombs
Maximum speed 256 mph
Range 830 miles

Fairey Barracuda (Britain)
This carrier bomber/torpedo bomber first flew in 1940 but development went ahead only from 1942 onwards. Embarked aboard the carriers of the British Pacific fleet, the Barracuda first saw action against the Japanese with an attack on enemy installations at Sabang, Sumatra, on 19 April 1944.

Mk I
Crew 3
Power plant 1 x Rolls Royce Merlin 30 in-line, 1260hp
Armament 2 x 0.303-in machine-guns, 2000lb of bombs or torpedo
Maximum speed 235 mph
Range 524 miles

Grumman F4F Wildcat
A symbol of the US Navy's defiance and will to fight back at the most testing time of the Pacific air war, the F4F put into that service's hands an effective, modern monoplane fighter, but only just in time.
The prototype XF4F-2 first flew in September 1937 but prolonged technical troubles delayed service entry until November 1940, the first carrier deployment taking place in March 1941. In October of that year the tubby little naval fighter was dubbed 'Wildcat', thus starting the unbroken 'cat' line from Grumman that continues today with the F-14 Tomcat.
When the Japanese offensive broke, less than 230 F4F-3 and F4F-3As had been delivered. Marine Wildcat pilots distinguished themselves in the defence of Wake Island and US Navy F4F pilots claimed their first victory on 1 February 1942 in the Gilberts.
During the Battle of Midway, the three fighter squadrons embarked aboard *Enterprise*, *Hornet* and *Yorktown* (VF-6, VF-8 and VF-3) all flew Wildcats.
In air combat against the Japanese Navy's Mitsubishi A6M2 Zero, the Wildcat proved slightly less manoeuvrable and lacked the edge in performance in terms of level speed, rate of climb and ceiling – but the Grumman fighter was better protected (from the F4F-3 model onwards, which had pilot armour and self-sealing fuel tanks) and harder hitting, with six 0.50-in machine-guns.
Experienced F4F pilots learned to shy away from dogfights with the Zero, relying on a manoeuvre known as the 'Thach Weave' developed by John S. Thach of the US Navy, in which two fighters flew in a repeated criss-cross pattern to cover each other's six o'clock position.
From mid-1943 onwards Wildcats were rapidly supplanted aboard the US Navy's fast carriers by F5F Hellcats. In the land-based

Marine squadrons they were replaced by F4U Corsairs. But FM-2s (as Wildcats built by General Motors were dubbed) continued to serve widely in the Pacific aboard escort carriers.
In October 1944, when US Army troops were landed on Leyte island in the Philippines, Wildcats flying from the escort carriers of Task Group 77 provided close air support for the landings and fought off attacking aircraft, including Kamikazes.
A total of 7825 Wildcats were built between 1937 and 1945 in a progressively developed range of sub-types.

F4F-4
Crew 1
Power plant Pratt & Whitney R-1830-86 radial, 1200hp
Armament 6 x 0.50-in machine-guns
Maximum speed 318mph
Range 770 miles

Grumman TBF Avenger
Grumman's famous carrier-based torpedo-bomber got off to a near-disastrous start in the Battle of Midway, but the type went on to prove itself the most dependable and successful of US Navy aircraft in the Pacific war, sinking a vast tonnage of Japanese naval and merchant shipping.
Designed by the team which produced the Wildcat, the XTBF-1 included such modern features as a large ventral weapons bay and a powered dorsal turret. It first flew in August 1941 and, from mid-1942, Avengers took part in all the major air-to-sea engagements in the Pacific, operating from fast and escort carriers. TBFs contributed to the sinking and damaging of the Japanese carriers *Hiyo*, *Chiyoada* and *Zuikaku* in the first Battle of the Philippine Sea. In the second Battle of the Philippine Sea, in October 1944, TBFs played their part in the sinking of the battleship *Musashi* and four carriers.

TBF-1
Crew 3
Power plant Wright R-2600-8, 1700hp
Armament 2 x 0.50-in machine-guns, 1 x 0.30-in machine-gun, 2000lb of bombs or torpedoes
Maximum speed 271 mph
Range 1450 miles

Grumman F6F Hellcat
The Hellcats earned a particular distinction as having the best kill-to-loss ratio of any fighter of World War II – the extraordinary figure of 19 to 1. Hellcat pilots were credited with 5156 victories, the overwhelming majority of them being scored by carrier-based units, for the loss of 270 F6Fs.
Design work on this follow-on to the Wildcat began in earnest in September 1940. Big production orders followed Pearl Harbor and before the first flight at Grumman's Bethpage Field on 26 June 1942. The first kill came over a year later when Lieutenant Richard Rosech of VF-6, flying from the fast new carrier *Independence*, claimed an air-to-air victory over Marcus Island.
During late 1943 and early 1944 the Hellcats of TF58 carriers severely mauled Japanese land-based aircraft in a series of attacks. In the first Battle of the Philippine Sea, the Hellcat pilots annihilated their opponents,

turning the one-sided fight into the 'Marianas Turkey Shoot'. Thereafter Hellcat squadrons fought in virtually every action on the road to Japan – off Formosa on 12-14 October 1944, in the second Battle of the Philippine Sea on 24-25 October 1944, on Iwo Jima in February 1945 and on Okinawa in March 1945. All the top-scoring US Navy carrier aces were Hellcat pilots.

Hellcats also equipped British Fleet Air Arm squadrons in the Pacific. Their first action against the Japanese was on 29 August 1944, when aircraft from HMS Indomitable made strikes on targets in Java. Nine Fleet Air Arm Hellcat squadrons were in action in the last year of the Pacific war.

F6F-3
Crew 1
Power plant Pratt and Whitney R-2800-10 radial, 2000hp
Armament 6 x 0.50-in machine-guns
Maximum speed 375 mph
Range 1590 miles

Grumman F7F Tigercat
Designed initially as a heavy single-seat carrier-fighter, the twin-engined Tigercat had a troubled development period. Although there were long drawn-out carrier qualification trials with the type from mid-1944 onwards, it arrived operationally in the Pacific – as a land-based night fighter – only at the very end of the conflict.

F7F-3
Crew 1
Power plant 2 x Pratt & Whitney R-2800 radials, 2100hp
Armament 4 x 20-mm cannon, 4000lb of bombs
Maximum speed 427 mhp
Range 1200 miles

Grumman F8F Bearcat
Representing the pinnacle of piston-engined carrier-fighter design, the F8F Bearcat was developed during 1944 as a highly capable successor to the Hellcat. The first deployment was aboard the USS Langley in August 1945. Langley and VF-19 equipped with Bearcats were on their way to the western Pacific when Japan surrendered. US Navy pilots never saw combat in the type.

F8F-1
Crew 1
Power plant Pratt & Whitney R-2800 radial, 2100hp
Armament 4 x 0.50-in machine-guns
Maximum speed 434 mph
Range 1105 miles

Hawker Hurricane
The RAF's most important fighter during the Battle of Britain in 1940, the rugged, easily repaired Hurricane shouldered the main burden of the Burma campaign of 1942-45, where its sturdy qualities once again came to the fore. The IIB and IIC were armed with 12 machine-guns and four 20-mm cannon. In Burma the IIC first saw service in 1943, initially as a night fighter, but soon found its most useful employment as a ground-attack aircraft. The Mk IV featured a 'universal armament wing' which could carry 40-mm cannon, drop tanks, bombs or rocket

projectiles. Production continued until September 1944.

IIB
Crew 1
Power plant 1 x Rolls Royce Merlin 20 in-line, 1280hp
Armament 12 x 0.303-in machine-guns
Maximum speed 340 mph
Range 460 miles

Lockheed PV-1/PV-2 Ventura/Harpoon
Developed from the Hudson medium bomber, the PV-1 entered service in late 1942 to provide the US Navy with a fast, well-armed patrol bomber for operations in areas where enemy fighter opposition might be encountered and lumbering flying boats would be too vulnerable. The improved PV-2, named Harpoon, had a fixed forward-firing armament as well as turret-mounted defensive weapons. For long-range anti-submarine operations depth charges and an additional bomb bay fuel tank could be carried, together with wing drop-tanks.

PV-2
Crew 4-5
Power plant 2 x Pratt & Whitney R-2800-31 radials, 2000hp
Armament 9 x 0.50-in machine-guns, 2500lb of bombs
Maximum speed 280 mph
Range 1260 miles

Lockheed P-38 Lightning
The P-38 was instantly recognizable with its twin-boom fuselage, chosen to accommodate the turbo-superchargers which boosted the engine power of this single-seat, twin-engine fighter aircraft, originally conceived in 1937 as a high-altitude interceptor. The aircraft came to excel, however, as a long-range tactical fighter. In the Pacific the type's long-leggedness put it in the forefront of the island-hopping campaign, where self-contained P-38 groups carried spares and ground crews in special cargo and personnel pods to enable newly captured airstrips to be made ready for use in a very short time.

The first truly combat-ready version was the P-38F, built from early 1942. The P-38G and the follow-on P-38H had more powerful engines and could carry a heavier bomb load in the fighter-bomber role. The most important version numerically was the P-38L, 3923 of which were built. The final version was the two-seat P-38M, a radar-equipped night fighter, which became operational in the closing weeks of the Pacific war.

One of the P-38's more extraordinary achievements was the interception and destruction, in April 1943, of Admiral Yamamoto's Mitsubishi G4M bomber-transport over the Solomons, a mission carried out by the 339th Fighter Squadron at a range of 550 miles from its Guadalcanal base.

The P-38 was very successful in the Pacific where it is claimed to have destroyed more Japanese aircraft than any other Allied type. The leading US ace of the war, Major Richard Bong, scored all his 40 victories flying P-38s against the Japanese. Fittingly, a P-38 was the first USAAF type to land in Japan after the surrender.

P-38L
Crew 1
Power plant 2 x Allison V-1710-111 in-line, 1425hp
Armament 1 x 20-mm cannon, 4 x 0.50-in machine-guns, 4000lb of bombs/rockets
Maximum speed 390 mph
Range 2260 miles

Lockheed C-69
Small numbers of militarized versions of the sinuously elegant Lockheed L-49 Constellation airliner served with US Air Transport Command. Operating on trans-Pacific air routes, they could fly from California to Honolulu in 12 hours.

Crew 4
Power plant 4 x Wright R-3350, 2150hp
Maximum speed 324 mph
Range 5000 miles

Martin B-26 Marauder
A fast medium bomber of exceptionally clean lines, the B-26 had a bad reputation among its crews because of its high landing speed and hence accident rate. Design alterations and a new training programme went a long way to cure the problem and the B-26 saw extensive service in the southwest Pacific. Some models had a reserve fuel tank fitted in the rear bomb bay for long-range missions.

B-26B
Crew 7
Power plant 2 x Pratt & Whitney R-2800-39 radials, 2000hp
Armament 12 x 0.5-in machine-guns, 3000lb of bombs
Maximum speed 282 mph
Range 1150 miles

North American B-25 Mitchell
The prototype of this famous medium bomber first flew in 1940. In December 1941 the aircraft made its operational debut when a B-25A sank a Japanese submarine off the US west coast. In April 1942 specially stripped B-25s with extra fuel tanks took off from the carrier USS Hornet to make the famous raid on Tokyo.

The tactical demands of the Pacific theatre led to the development of the B-25G and H models, which were modified with a solid nose mounting a very heavy armament of machine-guns and a 75-mm cannon for anti-armour and anti-shipping strikes. The J model saw the reintroduction of a transparent nose for the bomb-aimer's position. A total of 4318 of this type were built between 1943 and 1945, most being employed on low-level tactical missions in the Pacific theatre, but many were converted once again to accommodate gun-heavy ground-strike noses.

B-25H
Crew 5
Power plant 2 x Wright R-2600-13 radials
Armament 14 x 0.50-in machine-guns, 1 x 75-mm cannon, 3000lb of bombs
Maximum speed 275 mph
Range 1350 miles

North American P-51 Mustang
Perhaps the most effective combat aircraft of

the war, the P-51 Mustang combined exceptionally long range for a single-engine aircraft plus formidable combat power. The basic airframe featuring an advanced laminar flow wing was developed by North American in 1940 but it was the use of the Rolls Royce Merlin engine (built in the United States by Packard) which gave the aircraft such outstanding performance.

The P-51B model began operating with USAAF squadrons in Burma in early 1944. The P-51D model, which introduced the distinctive bubble cockpit canopy, was ideal for long-range fighter sweeps and bomber escort over the Pacific. After the capture of Iwo Jima, P-51s based on the island could escort Marianas-based B-29s on raids on Japan, while P-51s made the first fighter strikes on Tokyo itself on 7 April 1945. In the closing months of the war some USAAF fighter groups in the Pacific were re-equipped with the P-51H, the fastest Mustang variant of them all, capable of 487 mph at 25,000 feet.

P-51D
Crew 1
Power plant 1 x RR-Packard Merlin V-1650-7 inline, 1695hp
Armament 6 x 0.50-in machine-guns, 2000lb of bombs
Maximum speed 437 mph
Range 2080 miles

Northrop P-61 Black Widow
Designed as a dedicated night fighter, the two-seat P-61 was as large as a medium bomber with air-intercept radar mounted in the nose. Entering services in 1944 with the 18th Fighter Group in the South Pacific where it replaced the P-70 (the A-20 Havoc adapted for the night-fighter role), the Black Widow made its first kill in July of that year.

P-61B
Crew 2
Power plant 2 x Pratt & Whitney R-2800-65 radials, 2000hp
Armament 4 x 0.50-in machine-guns, 4 x 20-mm cannon
Maximum speed 366 mph
Range 610 miles

Republic P-47 Thunderbolt
This big, barrel-chested fighter was the heaviest single-engined fighter in the world when the prototype XP-47B first flew in May 1941. The deep fuselage accommodated a turbo-supercharger in the rear with its complex ducts and trunking, boosting the performance of the 18-cylinder Pratt & Whitney twin-row radial that gave the aircraft such high performance in spite of its weight. Developed through several models, from block 25 of the P47D model onwards, the Thunderbolt was fitted with an all-round vision bubble canopy.

P-47Ds of the RAF and USAAF served side by side in Burma excelling in ground-attack operations, building a solid reputation for survival in battle and stability as a gun platform. The P-47N was designed expressly for Pacific operations where long range was at a premium. The N-model had larger, strengthened 'wet' wing, bringing internal fuel capacity up to 1266 gallons and giving a range of 2350 miles. P-47Ns could escort B-29 Superfortresses all the way from Saipan to their targets in Japan.

P-47D
Crew 1
Power plant 1 x Pratt & Whitney R-2800-59 Double Wasp radial, 2000hp
Armament 8 x 0.50-in machine-guns, 2500lb of bombs
Maximum speed 429 mph
Range 950 miles

Supermarine Spitfire
A legendary aircraft, elegant and evocative yet full of design stretchability, although conceived in the mid-1930s the Spitfire still represented the pinnacle of piston-engine fighter design at the end of its development life. Not so adaptable to the harsh climatic conditions of Burma and the southwest Pacific as its great contemporary, the Hawker Hurricane, nevertheless the Spitfire played a big part in Britain's air war in the Pacific. Spitfires supported the 14th Army in Burma, repulsed Japanese attacks on Darwin, Australia, and fought in Borneo, the Solomon Islands and New Guinea. Seafire IIIs flew operationally from the carriers of the British Pacific Fleet right up to the end of the war, when the superlative Griffon-engine Seafire XV was replacing them.

Mk VIII
Crew 1
Power plant 1 x Merlin 61, 2600hp
Armament 4 x 20-mm cannon, 4 x 0.303-in machine-guns
Maximum speed 402 mph
Range 650 miles

Vickers Vildebeest
Dating from the mid-1930s and designed as a land-based torpedo-bomber for coast defence, the Vildebeest proved woefully obsolete by the outbreak of the Pacific war. Vildebeest pilots, however, fought bravely in the defence of Malaya and Java.

Mk IV
Crew 2
Power plant Bristol Perseus VIII, 810hp
Armament 2 x 0.303-in machine-guns, torpedo
Maximum speed 156 mph
Range 625 miles

Vought SB2U Vindicator
This scout bomber was approaching obsolescence on the outbreak of the Pacific war. A total of 167 reached the US Navy and Marines in 1939-40, some of which saw service at Midway.

Crew 2
Power plant Pratt & Whitney R-1350-02 Wasp radial, 750hp
Armament 2 x 0.30-in machine-guns, 1000lb of bombs
Maximum speed 243 mph
Range 700 miles

Vultee Vengeance
Designed to meet a 1940 RAF requirement for a dive-bomber, most of the 700 aircraft built served with the RAF and Indian Air Force in Burma, although some were operated by the USAAF as the A-35 in second-line roles. The RAAF also received some Vengeance Is.

Crew 2
Power plant Wright R-2600-13
Armament 4 x 0.50-in machine-guns, 1000lb of bombs
Maximum speed 279 mph
Range 600 miles

Japanese Aircraft

Navy

Aichi D3A1 'Val'
One of the aircraft types which led the strike on Pearl Harbor, the Aichi D3A dive-bomber first flew in 1937. Despite its obsolete appearance – a clumsy-looking aircraft with a fixed, spatted undercarriage – the D3A (or Navy Type 99 Carrier Bomber Model 11) was at the cutting edge of the Japanese tide of victories in 1941-2 and sank more Allied fighting ships than any other type of Axis aircraft. The aircraft was markedly manoeuvrable and could lift a 250-kg bomb on a swing-down, crutch mounting below the fuselage centre line, plus two underwing 60-kg bombs.

The dive-bombing efficiency of the carrier-borne D3A1 crews proved devastatingly effective in Japan's initial attacks, but the attrition of crews and carriers in 1942-3 meant that an increasing number of D3A1s operated from shore bases. In June 1942 a longer-range D3A2 version appeared. It was in action during the Philippine campaign of 1944 but losses were heavy.

Crew 2
Power plant (D3A2) 1 Mitsubishi Kinsei radial, 1070hp
Armament 3 x 7.7-mm machine-guns, 370kg of bombs
Maximum speed 266 mph
Range 970 miles

Aichi E13A 'Jake'
The most important Japanese floatplane of the war, the E13A three-seat reconnaissance aircraft operated from cruisers and seaplane tenders. Its exceptionally long endurance of 15 hours made it very useful in the scouting role. It was sometimes employed on bombing and shipping-attack missions.

Crew 3
Power plant Mitsubishi Kinsei radial, 1060hp
Armament 1 x 7.7-mm maching-gun
Maximum speed 234 mph
Range 1298 miles

Aichi E16A1 Zuiun 'Paul'
Designed as a successor to the E13A floatplane, the Zuiun (Auspicious Cloud) reconnaissance bomber entered service in late 1943. The aircraft's wings were designed to fold for stowage aboard cruisers and dive-brakes were incorporated into the front float struts. Many were lost in the 1944 Philippines fighting.

Crew 2
Power plant Mitsubishi MK8A Kinsei radial, 1300hp
Armament 3 x 7.7-mm machine-guns, 250kg of bombs
Maximum speed 273 mph
Range 1500 miles

Aichi B7A Ryusei 'Grace'

A big and technically ambitious aircraft, the B7A Ryusei (Shooting Star) was designed as a carrier-attack aircraft, capable of carrying both bombs and torpedoes. Destruction of the Japanese carrier fleet meant that the B7A1 and the improved B7A2 operated almost exclusively from land bases.

Crew 2
Power plant Nakajima Nk9C Homare radial, 1800hp
Armament 2 x 20-mm cannon, 1 x 7.7-mm machine-gun, 800kg of bombs or torpedoes
Maximum speed 352 mph
Range 1900 miles

Aichi M6A Seiran

A floatplane designed for operation from the very large I-400 class submarine, the M6A Seiran (Mountain Haze) had a complicated wing and tail folding system for stowage in a small watertight hangar. Plans were laid in 1945 to attack the lock-gates of the Panama Canal and then the US Navy base on Ulithi Atoll, using submarine-launched Seirans but the war ended before either attack could be made.

Crew 2
Power plant Aichi AE1P Atsuta inverted-vee in-line
Armament 1 x 13-mm machine gun, 800kg of bombs
Maximum speed 295 mph
Range 740 miles

Kawanishi E7K2 'Alf'

Obsolete when the Pacific war began, the E7K2 biplane reconnaissance floatplane nevertheless soldiered on in front-line service, on convoy protection or on anti-submarine patrol until 1943.

Crew 3
Power plant Mitsubishi Suisei radial, 870hp
Armament 3 x 7.7-mm machine-guns, 120kg of bombs

Kawanishi H6K 'Tillie'

A long-range patrol flying boat, the H6K first flew in 1936 and was developed in a range of improved versions until supplanted by the H8K from 1942 onwards. It was subsequently operated as a transport by the Navy and by Dai Nippon airways.

Crew 8, 10 passengers
Power plant 4 x Nakajima Hikari radials, 840hp each
Armament 3 x 7.7-mm machine-guns, 2 x 800kg of torpedoes or bombs
Maximum speed 210 mph
Range 2500 miles

Kawanishi H8K 'Emily'

Judged to be the best military flying boat of the war, the H8K had a powerful defensive armament and good protection for crew and fuel tanks, making it notoriously difficult for Allied fighters to shoot down, in spite of its apparent clumsiness.
Later models were fitted with retractable, stabilizing floats and a fully retracting dorsal turret. Transport versions could carry up to 64 men.

Crew 9
Power plant 4 x Mitsubishi Mk4A Kaseii radials, 1530hp
Armament 5 x 20-mm cannon, 5 x 7.7-mm machine-guns
Maximum speed 290 mph
Range 4475 miles

Kawanishi N1K1 Kyofu 'Rex'

One of the few floatplane fighters of the war, the N1K1 first became operational in 1942 and was designed to provide air cover for amphibious landing forces where no airstrip had been seized. The aircraft was well-armed and manoeuvrable but production was very limited, ceasing in 1944 in favour of the N1K1-J land plane fighter.

Crew 1
Power plant Mitsubishi MK4D Kasei radial, 1460hp
Armament 2 x 20-mm cannon, 2 x 7.7-mm machine-guns
Maximum speed 304 mph
Range 650 miles

Kawanishi N1K1-J Shiden/ N1K2-J Shiden-Kai 'George'

Considered by Allied pilots to be one of the best Japanese aircraft of the war, the NiK1-J was a private venture development of the Kyofu combat floatplane. First reaching naval fighter units in 1943, the N1K1 went some way to answering the Navy's pressing need for an aircraft capable of besting the US Navy's new Hellcats and Corsairs.
But it was a developed version, the N1K2-J Shiden-Kai, which proved to be a truly outstanding aircraft, capable of meeting the best Allied fighters on equal terms. In February 1945 Warrant Officer Kinsuke Moto single-handedly engaged 12 US Navy F5Fs in combat, shooting down four of them. A high-altitude version, the N1K5-J, was under development at the end of the war.

Crew 1
Power plant Nakajima NK9B Homare 1820hp
Armament (N1K2-J) 4 x 20-mm cannon
Maximum speed 363 mph
Range 890 miles

Mitsubishi A5M 'Claude'

The Japanese Navy's first 'modern' monoplane fighter, the prototype A5M first flew in 1935. The type was very successful in China but had been relegated to secondary roles by the eve of the Pacific war. From 1942 these aircraft served as fighter-trainers, the few remaining A5M4s being used in Kamikaze attacks.

Crew 1
Power plant (A5M4) Nakajima Kotobuki 41, 710hp
Armament 2 x 7.7-mm machine-guns
Maximum speed 280 mph
Range 750 miles

Mitsubishi G3M 'Nell'

Developed by the Navy in great secrecy, the Mitsubishi G3M showed how advanced was Japan's prewar air industry when, in August 1937, aircraft based on Formosa attacked targets in China 1250 miles distant, thus accomplishing the world's first trans-oceanic air attack. When met by effective fighter opposition over China, the Mitsubishi aircraft proved very vulnerable. Bombs were carried externally on racks under the fuselage.
G3M1 bombers with a smaller force of G4M1s led the attack on the British naval Task Force Z, sinking the battleship *Prince of Wales* and battlecruiser *Repulse* with bombs and torpedoes.
The aircraft evolved through improved versions, culminating in the very long-ranged G3M2. By 1943 the aircraft had been relegated to training and maritime reconnaissance, fitted with ASV radar. A transport version was known as the L3Y1 and codenamed 'Tina' by the Allies.

G3M1
Crew 5
Power plant 2 x Kinsei 2,825hp
Armament 3 x 7.7-mm machine-guns
Maximum speed 216 mph
Range 2300 miles

Mitsubishi F1M1 'Pete'

This two-seat observation floatplane equipped the catapult flights on battleships and cruisers of the Japanese Navy and on several seaplane tenders. The biplane's primary role was reconnaissance but in the early stages of the war it acted as a dive-bomber in support of assault landings and even as a fighter. Over 1000 were built.

Crew 2
Power plant Nakajima Hikari radial, 875hp
Armament 3 x 7.7-mm machine-guns, 250kg of bombs
Maximum speed 230 mph
Range 460 miles

Mitsubishi A6M Reisen (Zero-Sen) 'Zeke'

More than any other aircraft the 'Zero' symbolizes Japanese air power. It served the Japanese Navy from September 1940, when it first went into action over China, right to the very end of the Pacific war, when the last survivors hurled themselves at Allied warships in Kamikaze attacks.
The manoeuvrability and combat power of the Zero stunned Allied pilots when the Japanese offensive broke in December 1941. In spite of reports from China, the capabilities of this nimble, hard-hitting carrier fighter came as a complete surprise. Its long range gave the Japanese Navy a great strategic advantage, but that range was bought at the expense of lightness of construction and lack of armour protection or self-sealing fuel tanks. When the Japanese were forced on to the defensive, the Zero's shortcomings were shown up by a new generation of Allied carrier aircraft. Conceived out of the experience of air fighting in China, the first prototype A6M flew in April 1939. On the eve of the attack on Pearl Harbor, the Japanese Navy had a total of 521 carrier fighters on strength, of which 328 were A6M2s. It was predominantly these aircraft, both carrier- and land-based, which were the instrument by which Japan had effectively acquired superiority over the western Pacific, outclassing in air-to-air combat those few Allied fighters which had escaped being shot up on the ground.

By the end of 1942, however, the A6M2 and A6M3 were becoming outclassed by a new generation of Allied aircraft, although development and production of the Zero continued until the end of the war. The A6M5 could match the slightly less manoeuvrable Grumman F6F Hellcat in combat but was much more vulnerable to battle damage. In late 1943 the A6M5b model was introduced, at last incorporating some pilot-protecting armour and fire extinguishers for the fuel tanks, but even these features could not save inexperienced Japanese Navy pilots from a crushing defeat in the 1944 'Great Marianas Turkey Shoot'. Production continued right to the end, the last model to be developed being the A6M8, which had the forward fuselage redesigned to accommodate the 1650-hp Mitsubishi Kinsei radial. Two prototypes were tested and large production orders placed for the radically improved fighter, but Japanese industry was crumbling under the strain of US bombing, made worse by chronic shortages of raw materials. When A6M production finally came to a halt, 10,449 A6Ms had been built by Mitsubishi and Nakajima.

A6M5
Crew 1
Power plant Nakajima NK1F Sakae radial, 1130hp
Armament 2 x 20-mm cannon, 2 x 7.7-mm machine-guns
Maximum speed 350 mph
Range 1190 miles

Mitsubishi G4M 'Betty'

Development of the G4M as a land-based Japanese Navy attack bomber with exceptional speed and range requirements began in 1937. Its long range, in particular, made it very effective in the opening rounds of the Pacific war, enabling it to fly far over the Pacific from northern Australia to the Aleutian Islands.
Like its great contemporary, the Zero, the G4M acquired range at the expense of vulnerability. The wings contained huge but completely unprotected, integral fuel tanks and inside the fat, cigar-shaped fuselage there were more tanks. The defensive armament was inadequate and there was no armour protection for the crew.
When the Japanese were forced on to the defensive, the range capability of the G4M became less strategically important and the bomber proved an easy prey for Allied fighters. A few hits and the aircraft would burn, earning itself the macabre nickname the 'Flying Lighter'.
Attempts to remedy this deficiency were made by means of progressive design modifications. The G4M1 introduced CO2 fire-extinguishers for the fuel tanks and a 20-mm cannon rear armament. The G4M2, powered by twin 1800-hp Mitsubishi Kasei 21 radial engines, featured a new laminar-flow wing, together with other aerodynamic improvements and a 20-mm cannon in a powered dorsal turret.
A number of G4M2s were modified, their bomb-bay doors being removed, to carry and launch the Ohka, piloted Kamikaze missile. These aircraft, designated G4M2e, were heavy and had poor handling characteristics when carrying the Ohka, and were very vulnerable to Allied fighter attack. On March 21 1945 16 bombers taking part in the first

Ohka mission were shot out of the air before they could even get their piloted bombs to the launch point.

G4M1
Crew 7
Power plant 2 x Mitsubishi MK4A Kasei 11, 1530hp
Armament 1 x 20-mm cannon, 5 x 7.7-mm machine guns
Maximum speed 266 mph
Range 3750 miles

Mitsubishi J2M Raiden 'Jack'

Designed and manufactured by the team responsible for the A6M Zero, the J2M Raiden (Thunderbolt), also intended for the Japanese Navy, had a completely different tactical purpose. It was a short-range point defence interceptor, designed to have a phenomenal rate of climb and high speed but with only limited range and endurance. Built round a high-performance Mitsubishi Kasei 13 radial engine, the prototype's airframe was optimized for high speed but had to be adapted to tactical practicalities. From its first flight in March 1942 development of the aircraft was dogged by problems. The most-built version, the J2M3, entered service in 1944 with four wing-mounted cannon, but still had inadequate high-altitude performance to meet the US Army Air Force bombers that were beginning to pound the homeland. The J2M5 version incorporated a three-stage supercharger and demonstrated a maximum speed of 382 mph at 22,310 feet, but there were too few of these potent bomber-destroyers to ward off the inevitable. Plagued by technical problems and indecision by the Navy as to its relative production importance, the Raidens were, when the final test came, too few and too late.

J2M3
Crew 1
Power plant Mitsubishi MK4C Kasei, 1800hp
Armament 4 x 20-mm cannon
Maximum speed 365 mph
Range 1180 miles

Nakajima B5N 'Kate'

At the outset of the Pacific war, the Nakajima B5N2, equipping Japanese Navy aircraft carriers, represented the state of the art in torpedo-bombers. As a land-based attack bomber the B5N1 had gone into action in China, where it had proved markedly successful. The B5N2 version, which entered production in 1940, featured a double-row Sakae radial engine, and this was the variant that spearheaded the torpedo attacks on the US Pacific Fleet at Pearl Harbor. In the following 12 months B5N2s delivered fatal blows to three US aircraft carriers. Outclassed and very vulnerable, but not replaced as a front-line, naval strike aircraft until late 1944, the B5N2 had a renewed lease of life as an anti-submarine convoy escort, operating in areas where Allied fighters could not reach.

B5N2
Crew 3
Power plant Nakajima Sakae 11, 1000hp
Armament 1 x 7.7-mm machine-guns, 800kg of bombs or torpedo
Maximum speed 235 mph
Range 1230 miles

Nakajima J1N Gekko 'Irving'

The J1N Gekko (Moonlight) began life in 1941 as a prototype long-range escort fighter but production plans were shelved because of its excessive technical complexity and inadequate manoeuvrability when pitted in trials against single-engined fighters. It was redesigned as a reconnaissance aircraft (J1N1-C), but production continued at a low level until in 1943 field modifications to the type as an improvised night fighter, with twin, upward-firing 20-mm cannon in the observer's rear cockpit, proved successful. Series production of the dedicated J1N1-S night-fighter began in August 1943 and some aircraft were fitted with airborne intercept (AI) radar in the nose, sometimes additionally with a small searchlight. In night-fighter operations the Gekko proved effective against the comparatively slow B-24 but not against the faster B-29. Production ended in December 1944.

J1N1-S
Crew 2
Power plant 2 x Nakajima Nk1F Sakae 21, 1130hp
Armament 4 x 20-mm cannon
Maximum speed 315 mph
Range 1580 miles

Nakajima B6N Tenzan 'Jill'

Intended as a replacement for the B5N, the Tenzan (Heavenly Mountain) drew largely on the aerodynamics of the earlier aircraft but with a much more powerful Nakajima Mamoru engine.
Teething troubles with the Mamoru slowed development and the aircraft did not pass carrier acceptance trials until 1943, but its high landing speed restricted its use to the Japanese Navy's remaining large carriers. From 1943 the aircraft was built with the Mitsubishi Kasei engine as the B6N2. During the battle of the Marianas, the B6N2's first major engagement, it failed to achieve any significant results when stripped of fighter cover. The type was operational to the end, being particularly heavily engaged in the fighting for Okinawa, making both conventional and suicide attacks on US warships.

B6N2
Crew 3
Power plant Mitsubishi MK4T Kasei 25, 1850hp
Armament 2 x 7.7-mm machine-guns, 800kg of bombs or torpedo
Maximum speed 300 mph
Range 1085 miles

Nakajima C6N Saiun 'Myrt'

Designed to a very demanding specification for a carrier-borne reconnaissance aircraft with exceptional range and high speed, the Saiun (Painted Cloud) first saw action in 1944. With a range of 3000 miles it proved highly useful to the Japanese Navy, being able to shadow the US fleet while almost immune from fighter interception. A few C6Ns were converted as night fighters for home defence in the last months of the war.

C6N1
Crew 3
Power plant Nakajima NK9-B Homare 11 radial, 1820hp

Armament 1 x 7.9-mm machine-gun
Maximum speed 379 mph
Range 3300 miles

Yokosuka D4Y Suisei 'Judy'

The Suisei (Comet) was designed as a naval carrier-based dive-bomber, and small numbers of this fast, elegant-looking machine, powered by an in-line, liquid-cooled engine, became operational from late 1942 onwards. But they had little impact on the course of the naval war, large numbers being shot down in the 'Great Marianas Turkey Shoot', when they failed to hit a single US carrier. A single-seat version, specially designed for Kamikaze attacks, was produced in 1945 as the D4Y4 Special Attack Bomber.

D4Y2
Crew 2
Power plant Aichi, inverted-V in-line, 1200hp
Armament 3 x 7.7-mm machine-guns, 560kg of bombs
Maximum speed 360 mph
Range 790 miles

Yokosuka P1Y Ginga 'Frances'

The Ginga (Milky Way) medium bomber was designed to replace the G3M 'Nell' in the Japanese Navy's line-up from 1943 onwards, but appeared in action only in the spring of 1945. It was fast and capable. Some aircraft were converted to the night-fighter role.

P1Y1
Crew 3
Power plant 2 x Nakajima NK9B Homare radials, 1820hp
Armament 2 x 20-mm cannon, 1000kg of bombs or torpedo
Maximum speed 340 mph
Range 4000 miles

Yokosuka MXY7 Ohka

This tiny, rocket-propelled suicide aircraft was in essence a powered bomb with control surfaces guided by an on-board computer – a volunteer Kamikaze pilot. Named Navy Suicide Attacker Ohka (Cherry Blossom), the weapon was designed to be air-launched at stand-off range against important surface targets.
A US destroyer was sunk off Okinawa on 12 April 1945 by Ohka attack, but the lumbering mother planes proved highly vulnerable on the run-in and production of the rocket-powered Type 11 was halted.
Development of a turbojet-powered model, to be launched from the Yokosuka P1Y fast bomber, was under way as the war ended, as were variants to be launched by catapult from submarines or from coastal caves.

Type 11
Crew 1
Power plant 3 x Type 4 rockets, 800-kg thrust for 10 seconds
Armament 1200-kg warhead
Maximum speed 403 mph
Range 23 miles

Army Air Force

Kawasaki Ki-45 Toryu 'Nick'

The Toryu (Dragon Killer) long-range, twin-engine fighter was heavily armed and well protected. It was a good defensive instrument, effective against far-ranging US Army Air Force B-24 bombers by day and, fitted with radar, in the front line of defence against B-29 raids on the Japanese homeland.

KAId
Crew 2
Power plant 2 x Nakajima Ha-25 radials, 970hp
Armament 2 x 20-mm, 1 x 30-mm cannon, 1 x 7.92-mm machine gun
Maximum speed 335 mph
Range 1240 miles

Kawasaki Ki-48 'Lily'

This light bomber was in the forefront of attacks on US and British forces when the Pacific air war began. Relatively slow and with a poor defensive armament, the type proved increasingly ineffective until production ended in mid-1944. Most survivors were expended around Okinawa in suicide attacks.

Ki-48-I
Crew 4
Power plant 2 x Nakajima Has-115 radial, 1130hp
Armament 3 x 7.7-mm machine guns, 400kg of bombs
Maximum speed 298 mph
Range 1230 miles

Kawasaki Ki-61 Hien 'Tony'

Very un-Japanese in concept, the Ki-61 was powered by a liquid-cooled, in-line twelve-cylinder inverted-V engine derived from a Daimler-Benz design. The Hien (Swallow) provided the Army Air Force with a fast, powerfully armed fighter, stronger and better protected than its contemporaries. It was, however, beset with production and maintenance problems which limited its operational career.
The Ki-61-I and its follow-on, Ki-61-I Kai, saw action in New Guinea in the 1944 Philippines campaign, over Formosa and Okinawa and in the final defence of the Japanese islands, where the type met B-29s, US Navy carrier aircraft, and later P-51 Mustangs flying from Iwo Jima.

Ki-61-Ia
Crew 1
Power plant Kawasaki Ha-40 inverted V-12, 1100hp
Armament 2 x 12.7-mm machine-guns, 2 x 20-mm cannon
Maximum speed 368 mph
Range 684 miles

Kawasaki Ki-100

A redesign of the in-line-engined Ki-61 to take a 1500-hp Kawasaki double-row radial, the resulting aircraft proved an outstanding fighter, equally suited to intercepting B-29s at high altitude or to hand-to-hand fighting with carrier-based Hellcats. Even the rawest, most inexperienced pilot had a fighting chance of survival in this exceptional machine.

Ki-100-II
Crew 1
Power plant Mitsubishi Ha 33, 1500hp

Armament 3 x 20-mm cannon, 12 x 12.7-mm machine-guns
Maximum speed 360 mph
Range 1367 miles

Kawasaki Ki-102 'Randy'

A derivative of the Ki-96 optimized for ground attack, Ki-102s in small numbers were committed to the struggle for Okinawa.

Ki-102b
Crew 2
Power plant 2 x Mitsubishi Ha-112-II radials, 1500hp
Armament 1 x 57-mm cannon, 2 x 20-mm cannon, 1 x 12.7-mm machine-gun
Maximum speed 360 mph
Range 1240 miles

Kokusai Ki-76 'Stella'

A parasol monoplane with a large wing fitted with extensive, Fowler-type flaps, the Ki-76 liaison and observation aircraft had good STOL characteristics. It served as an artillery spotter and aboard ship as an anti-submarine patrol aircraft.

Crew 2
Power plant Hitachi Ha-42 radial, 310hp
Armament 1 x 7.7-mm machine-gun
Maximum speed 111 mph
Range 460 miles

Mitsubishi Ki-21 'Sally'

The Ki-21 was the Japanese army's most important bomber at the outbreak of war, already battle-proven in China. Although progressively outclassed when faced by Allied fighters, it continued in front-line service until the Japanese surrender.

Ki-21-II bombers supported army ground operations in Thailand, Burma, Malaya and the Netherlands East Indies, and played an important part in the fall of the British possessions of Hong Kong and Rangoon. However, when they met Flying Tiger P-40s over China or RAF Hurricanes over Burma they suffered heavy losses. The long dorsal 'greenhouse' was replaced by a turret, activated by chain drive and bicycle pedals.

By the last year of the war the Ki-21 had been relegated to transport or special missions, such as the airborne commando attack launched from crash-landing Ki-21s on Yontan airfield, Okinawa.

Ki-21-I
Crew 5
Power plant 2 x Nakajima Ha-5 radials, 850hp
Armament 6 x 7.7-mm machine-guns
Maximum speed 268 mph
Range 932 miles

Mitsubishi Ki-30 'Ann'

An important participant in the air war in China, the Ki-30 light bomber first became operational in 1938. The Royal Thai Air Force operated the type against the French in January 1941. Some Ki-30s were committed to the Philippines after US aircraft had been driven off.
Crew 2
Power plant Mitsubishi Ha-6 radial, 850hp
Armament 2 x 7.7-mm machine-guns, 400kg of bombs

Maximum speed 263 mph
Range 1050 miles

Mitsubishi Ki-46-II 'Dinah'
This high-speed reconaissance aircraft made extensive clandestine flights over Southeast Asia on the eve of the Pacific war.
Its exceptional altitude performance made it almost immune to interception and the type remained operational until the very end of the war. It was also designed as a ground-attack aircraft and improvised interceptor (Ki-46-III Kai).

Crew 2
Power plant 2 x Mitsubishi Ha-102 radials, 1050hp
Armament 1 x 7.7-mm machine-gun
Maximum speed 375 mph
Range 1530 miles

Mitsubishi Ki-51 'Sonia'
Straightforwardly engineered and with a fixed undercarriage, the Ki-51 ground-attack aircraft was technically obsolete by the start of the Pacific war but was kept in production because of its ease of maintenance and operability from austere forward airstrips. Remarkably, a new production line was opened in 1944. Most survivors were sacrificed as suicide aircraft.

Crew 2
Power plant Mitsubishi Ha-26 radial, 900hp
Armament 3 x 7.7-mm machine-guns, 200kg of bombs
Maximum speed 363 mph
Range 660 miles

Mitsubishi Ki-57 'Topsy'
The Japanese army's standard personnel transport aircraft was based on an airliner derivation of the Ki-21 bomber. Ki-57s were used for the Japanese paratroop attack on Palembang on 14 February 1942. The type was also used by the Japanese Navy and Dai Nippon airline.

Crew 4, 11 soldiers
Power plant 2 x Nakajima Ha-5 KAI radials, 850hp
Armament none
Maximum speed 267 mph
Range 932 miles

Mitsubishi Ki-67 Hiryu 'Peggy'
A very effective medium bomber, the Hiryu (Flying Dragon) appeared in combat at a time when the Allies were regaining overall air superiority. It was well protected and remarkably manoeuvrable and could carry 800kg of bombs or torpedoes. Some were acquired by the Navy and aircraft of both Navy and Army Air Forces made repeated torpedo attacks on US shipping. In its original role as a bomber the Hiryu operated in China and, from a base on Iwo Jima, units made repeated strikes against B-29 bases in the Marianas.
The Ki-109 was a derivative, armed with a 75-mm cannon in the nose as an improvised bomber destroyer.

Crew 6
Power plant 2 x Mitsubishi Ha-214 radials

Armament 2 x 7.92-mm machine-guns, 2 x 12.7-mm machine-guns, 1 x 20-mm cannon
Maximum speed 334 mph
Range 1740 miles

Nakajima Ki-27
The Japanese Army Air Force's first 'modern' monoplane fighter, the Ki-27 still owed something to the past, with its fixed undercarriage and emphasis on manoeuvrability. In March 1938 the fighter went into action over China and quickly displayed its superiority. In the Russo-Japanese fighting of summer 1939, the Ki-27 proved the master in a dogfight with Soviet I-15 fighter biplanes but could be matched by the I-16 monoplane if the Soviet pilots avoided close-quarter engagements. Committed to battle in the opening moves of the Pacific war in Burma and Malaya, the Ki-27 was progressively relegated to home defence, and then to advanced training. It equipped the front-line squadrons of the Manchukuo air force throughout. In the last months of the war some were used as Kamikaze aircraft with a 500-kg bombload.

Crew 1
Power plant 1 x Nakajima Ha-1 radial, 650hp
Armament 2 x 7.7 machine-guns
Maximum speed 292 mph
Range 390 miles

Nakajima Ki-43 Hayabusa 'Oscar'
The Hayabusa (Peregrine Falcon) Army Air Force fighter came as almost as great a shock as the carrier-based Zero to the Allies, whose intelligence had sorely underestimated the technical ability of the Japanese aircraft industry. The Ki-43 was numerically the Japanese Army Air Force's most important fighter and remained in service from the beginning to the final campaigns of the Pacific War.
Production of the Army Type 1 Fighter Model 1A Hayabusa began in March 1941. The type proved highly manoeuvrable but underarmed and, with the advent of ever stiffer Allied fighter opposition, an improved Ki-43-II model with armour protection for the pilot and self-sealing fuel tanks was introduced.

Ki-43-II
Crew 1
Power plant Nakajima Ha-115 radial, 1150hp
Armament 2 x 12.7-mm machine-guns
Maximum speed 331 mph
Range 995 miles

Nakajima Ki-44 Shoki 'Tojo'
The Ki-44 Shoki (Devil-Queller) provided the Japanese Army Air Force with an effective, fast-climbing, point-defence interceptor. Shokis were based in Japan after the Doolittle raids on Japanese cities. They were also stationed in China, Burma and Malaya, and guarded the vital Sumatra oilfields. The Ki-44-II featured four 20-mm cannon. Production was ended in late 1944, the Shoki being supplanted by the Ki-84.

Crew 1
Power plant Nakajima Ha-41 radial, 1250hp
Armament 4 x 12.7-mm machine-guns
Maximum speed 360 mph
Range 575 miles

Nakajima Ki-49 Donryu 'Helen'
Designed as a replacement for the Ki-21 bomber, early production Donryus (Storm Dragon) made attacks on New Guinea and northern Australia. The type did not offer much improvement in either performance or bombload over the earlier plane, although it was better protected.
After US forces invaded the Philippines Donryu units were heavily committed, suffering severe losses until the end of 1944 when the survivors were switched to suicide missions. Some aircraft operated as troop transports, others as improvised night-fighters.

Ki-49IIa
Crew 8
Power plant 2 x Nakajima Ha-109 radials, 1500hp
Armament 5 x 7.7-mm machine-guns, 1 x 20-mm cannon
Maximum speed 306 mph
Range 1243 miles

Nakajima Ki-84 Hayate 'Frank'
The Hayate (Gale) was the finest Japanese fighter of the war – fast, manoeuvrable and as combat-worthy as any Western equivalent. The first prototype flew in April 1943 and the first service trial batch impressed Army Air Force pilots who by now had begun to appreciate the advantage of high speed and a good degree of pilot and fuel tank protection. The type was flown by an experimental squadron against the US 14th Air Force in China, which sent back alarming reports of a formidable new Japanese fighter.
In addition to excelling as an interceptor and penetrating fighter, the aircraft was used as a fighter-bomber and even as a dive-bomber. The Hayate was simple to fly – a saving grace for the young, inexperienced pilots put into the line with inadequate flying hours' experience. There were some handling quirks, however: ground handling was generally poor but climb rate and manoeuvrability were excellent, providing the type with an edge even over such formidable US types as the P-47N and P-51H. In the Philippines ten sentai (squadrons) fought desperately to hold the US invaders in the decisive battles around Leyte but, although they were formidable in the air, lack of spares and maintenance problems lessened their usefulness as much as combat losses.
The type was powered by a succession of Ha 45-series engines. There was a consistent technical problem with low fuel pressure which was never fully fixed, and production was crippled by B-29 raids on the Musashi engine plant and on Nakajima's own airframe assembly unit. A dispersal programme kept production going during 1945.
Several versions of the Ki-84 were proposed in the last year of the war, including a high-altitude interceptor (Ki-117) and an all-wooden airframe variant (Ki-106).

Ki-84-Ia
Crew 1
Power plant Nakajima Ha-45 radial, 1900hp
Armament 3 x 12.7-mm machine-guns, 2 x 20-mm cannon
Maximum speed 392 mph
Range 1053 miles

INDEX

Page numbers in **bold** refer to an illustration

ACKNOWLEDGEMENTS

The Hamlyn Publishing Group Limited would like to thank the following individuals and organizations for their kind permission to reproduce the photographs and colour profiles appearing in this book.

Aerospace Publishing Ltd   Robert L. Lawson   Imperial War Museum   MacClancy Collection   United States Air Force   United States Navy   United States Marine Corps

Book design: Hussain R. Mohamed